Raising Kids and Teens with FASD

of related interest

Life in the FASD Lane
Rossi's Fabulous Guide to Navigating Your Teens and Young Adulthood
Rossi Griffin
Illustrated by Tim Stringer
ISBN 978 1 80501 418 8
eISBN 978 1 80501 419 5

The A–Z of Therapeutic Parenting: Strategies and Solutions
Sarah Naish
ISBN 978 1 78592 376 0
eISBN 978 1 78450 732 9
Audio ISBN 978 1 52937 496 4

Raising Kids with Big, Baffling Behaviors
Brain-Body-Sensory Strategies That Really Work
Robyn Gobbel
ISBN 978 1 83997 428 1
eISBN 978 1 83997 429 8
Audio ISBN 978 1 39981 631 1

The Complete Guide to Therapeutic Parenting
A Helpful Guide to the Theory, Research and What it Means for Everyday Life
Jane Mitchell and Sarah Naish
ISBN 978 1 78775 376 1
eISBN 978 1 78775 377 8
Audio ISBN 978 1 52936 518 4

Raising Kids and Teens with FASD

Advice and Strategies to Help Your Family to Thrive!

BARB CLARK

Foreword by Rebecca Tillou

Jessica Kingsley Publishers
London and Philadelphia

First published in Great Britain in 2026 by Jessica Kingsley Publishers
An imprint of John Murray Press

6

Front cover image source: Shutterstock®. The cover image is for illustrative purposes only, and any person featuring is a model.

A CIP catalogue record for this title is available from the British Library and the Library of Congress

ISBN 978 1 80501 390 7
eISBN 978 1 80501 391 4

Printed and bound in the United States by Integrated Books International

Jessica Kingsley Publishers' policy is to use papers that are natural, renewable and recyclable products and made from wood grown in sustainable forests. The logging and manufacturing processes are expected to conform to the environmental regulations of the country of origin.

Jessica Kingsley Publishers
Carmelite House
50 Victoria Embankment
London EC4Y 0DZ

www.jkp.com

John Murray Press
Part of Hodder & Stoughton Ltd
An Hachette Company

The authorised representative in the EEA is Hachette Ireland, 8 Castlecourt Centre, Dublin 15, D15 XTP3, Ireland (email: info@hbgi.ie)

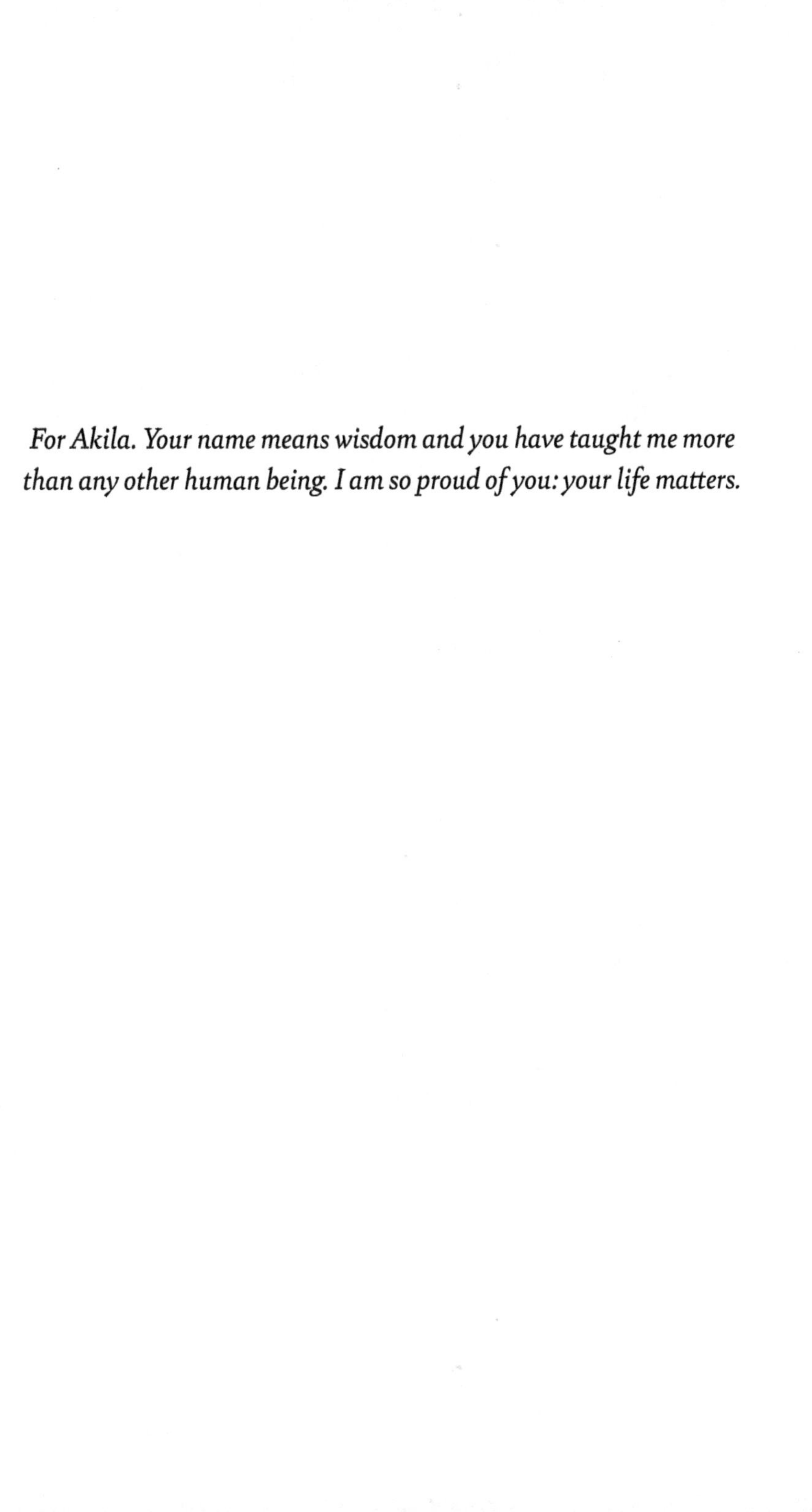

For Akila. Your name means wisdom and you have taught me more than any other human being. I am so proud of you: your life matters.

Contents

Foreword

Fate is a funny thing.

The Merriam-Webster Dictionary defines *fate* as "the will or principle or determining cause by which things in general are believed to come to be as they are or events to happen as they do." I believe that *fate* led Barb Clark's and my minds and souls to collide.

I entered the world of fetal alcohol spectrum disorder (FASD) in 2014. Barb had been in the FASD community for a few years before me and I had seen her name on social media platforms for FASD. I had heard her name in discussions about her being a parent of someone with FASD, who was teaching other parents, educators and doctors how to navigate the child and adolescent with FASD. She seemed like a powerful woman. I first met her in person at an FASD United Gala in Washington, D.C. She has such poise, and yet is casual, and has a way with words. Everyone who meets her leaves with a smile, knowledge, and, most importantly, *hope*.

I was diagnosed with FASD at 34 years old, and the hope I have for my future, and all of the tips and tricks I have learned from Barb for my own well-being, are priceless. Barb has taught me that my voice is invaluable. She has given me strength and confidence to speak out about my successes, but also my struggles, especially the ones most people do not want to talk about. The response to speaking out has been phenomenal, all because Barb took me in, and believed in me.

Raising Kids and Teens with FASD brings out who Barb Clark really is. It tells the true tales of her parenting a child with FASD—"true tales" meaning not only the ones that happened without an issue. She deep dives into life's events that show her frustration at FASD, and how she thinks outside the box to regulate dire sensory needs, for example, dancing outside her car, on a road, to de-escalate what could have been an unsafe situation for all involved. This book reveals Barb's first-hand knowledge of how an FASD brain works. She details how, when her daughter was diagnosed with FASD, Barb immersed herself in everything FASD. Her daughter's brain worked differently, and wonderfully, and Barb wanted a front row seat.

Raising Kids and Teens with FASD is a book for parents who want to understand their child with FASD. Barb breaks down medical jargon into concrete, real-life examples her family went through with her daughter. The "Aha!" moments throughout this book for me were many. People ask for the differences between attention deficit hyperactivity disorder, autism, and FASD. Barb gets into it! Her personal stories make understanding the brain of those with FASD easier. She touches on diagnostics and the FASD world. She gives such wonderful ideas and insight.

There is not a plethora of books in this world on FASD. Many are filled with doctor jargon and are hard to read. When you are a parent, or a person living with FASD, you want to read a book that feels as if you are on a coffee date with the author. *Raising Kids and Teens with FASD* is that book. Barb is your date. This book isn't all about everything Barb did right in raising her child with FASD—not at all. She tells you the stories that left her crying in her bedroom at night, because what she tried and thought would work to calm her child down did not. She recounts a tale of a blankie and a trash can. She discusses her mistakes, but she also discusses her triumphs. She needs to. We all do.

Every one of us messes up. Barb teaches us that messes are learning opportunities. They may not seem like it at the time, but they are. Those with FASD are also some of the best teachers. Barb learns through her daughter every day.

Raising Kids and Teens with FASD is a guide to surviving FASD. Whether you are a parent, an educator, a doctor, or a person living with FASD, this book is one to carry everywhere with you. As Barb states in the book, "We do better when we know better."

Rebecca Tillou, author of Tenacity, *and an adult living with FASD*

Preface

Barb

My first career was working with teenagers, and I truly loved it. Some of the youth I most enjoyed working with were the ones with big behaviors—the ones who would curse at me and challenge me. Years later, I found myself dealing with similar behaviors from my own daughter, and it wasn't as enjoyable. The difference between leaving work after eight hours and living with hard behaviors day in and day out is immense.

Back then, I believed that behavioral issues were intentional and often the result of poor parenting. My husband and I used to watch parents in stores and judge them when their child had a meltdown. Then we became parents, and none of the strategies our parents had used—or the ones I learned in my youth development program at university—worked with one of our children in particular.

Desperate for help, we sought advice from professionals, only to be dismissed. We were told we were paranoid and were advised to be more strict, but nothing worked. We assumed a loving, consistent, and structured environment would be enough for our children to thrive. It wasn't. Much too late, our oldest daughter was diagnosed with fetal alcohol spectrum disorder (FASD), something we knew almost nothing about.

Even after the diagnosis, we struggled to find effective ways to parent her. Eventually, I began working in the field of FASD, supporting families and training professionals. Over time, I realized that our story was not unique. Almost every family I worked with described the same exhausting journey to diagnosis—one marked by years of missteps, missed opportunities, misdiagnoses, and misunderstandings. Even after receiving a diagnosis, most caregivers found themselves stuck on a hamster wheel, using conventional parenting strategies that only led to frustration.

I became passionate about learning everything I could about FASD and committed to helping families and professionals better understand this hidden disability. My goal is to help individuals with FASD thrive and build stronger relationships with their loved ones. For that to happen, more professionals must develop greater competency in recognizing and addressing it. I worked for a few years for an FASD support organization called Proof Alliance.

Although this book is written with caregivers in mind, I hope professionals will read it as well and apply these strategies in their work—not only with children but also with the caregivers who support them. This book is for all families raising a child prenatally exposed to alcohol, whether biological, foster, adoptive, or kinship caregivers. FASD is one of the most stigmatized disabilities, with blame often directed at birth parents who used alcohol during pregnancy. This stigma must end.

I currently run my own FASD-focused coaching, training, and consulting business. For nearly a decade, I served as the Director of Training for Families Rising, a North American organization dedicated to child welfare. Each year, I train thousands of professionals and caregivers on understanding and supporting individuals with Fetal Alcohol Spectrum Disorders (FASD). I am also the head coach for the FASD Success Caregiver Kickstart Program, an international virtual coaching program supporting caregivers. Over the years, I've worked with countless families raising children with FASD and have learned so much from them. Their dedication and hard work inspire me daily.

Most of all, I've learned from individuals with FASD, including my amazing daughter Akila, who you'll meet throughout this book. Akila has given me permission to share some very personal and raw stories. Her resilience, strength, and willingness to be vulnerable are qualities I deeply admire. I am grateful to her and to my other children for allowing me to share our journey so that other families can do better.

Many families I've worked with over the years have allowed me to share their stories and allowed me to include them here. While names and details have been changed to protect their identities, their experiences offer invaluable lessons.

To the caregivers reading this, I say this often: think about how hard it is to care for these incredible kids. Now imagine how much harder it is for them to live with this brain injury every single day. This doesn't mean there isn't hope—without hope, I'd be a puddle on the floor. I've seen my own daughter thrive with the right supports, and I know your children can too.

The most important message I can share—whether you are a caregiver, professional, extended family member, or someone else in the life of a person with FASD—is this: It's up to us to be the change. We need to stop focusing on "fixing" these kids and instead shift our attention to creating environments where they can thrive. These individuals aren't broken—they are navigating a world that wasn't built with their unique needs in mind. Instead of asking, "What's wrong with them?" we need to start asking, "What happened to them?" and more importantly, "What can *we* do differently?

Akila

I have had a good life, but there have been many challenges. I am glad that my mom is able to share our challenges so that other families will not struggle as much as we did. I want other kids and adults who have FASD to have a good life and to learn from my mistakes, and my mom's mistakes (she made a lot—LOL).

Growing up with a brain injury is not easy. It has been hard. But I have also had a lot of good things happen to me. I am thankful to my first family for creating me. I wish I had not been exposed to alcohol, but I do not blame my first mom for that. She did not do it on purpose. I am also grateful for my adoptive family. I have really awesome siblings.

My mom and dad are the best. I like to call my mom "Bertha" and she calls me "Agnus"—it is our funny joke. My dad and I call each other "Sista Girl"—it is our inside joke. I am grateful for all they have done for me, and I am proud of myself.

I have been through a lot in my life and I keep getting back up. Mom always says that I am a very tough woman, and I agree with her.

People who have FASD are not bad people, we just have different brains from others. We are smart and we want to have good lives. But most people do not understand us.

I am really glad my mom wrote this book and I hope that it helps you. Thank you for taking the time to learn more about FASD.

Chapter 1

Meet Our Family

A life-changing day: Meeting Akila

September 9, 1999, will forever be etched in my memory as one of the most transformative days of my life. It was the day we met Akila, our eldest daughter, and the day she became part of our family. At just five weeks old, she was a tiny bundle of wonder, radiating innocence and possibility. The day was perfect—it was a bright sunny day, full of hope, and marked by the kind of joy that can never truly be captured in words. We had driven all the way from Minnesota to Georgia to meet her, and after signing the final papers, we were officially her parents.

The journey back home was long—an 18-hour drive—but it felt like the blink of an eye. I sat in the back seat of our 1997 Honda Civic, staring at her for hours, marveling at the idea that she was now ours. The world outside the car seemed to blur away, and I was overwhelmed by the surreal beauty of the moment. Akila was so small, so perfect, and she filled our hearts with a love we hadn't known was possible.

Adoption as a calling

Michael and I had always known that adoption would play a role in our lives. Long before we even said "I do," we dreamed of building a family that included both biological and adopted children. But as life unfolded, the biological option wasn't meant to be. Instead of grieving what we couldn't have, we leaned into what we could. Adoption wasn't Plan B—it was simply a different path to the family we had always envisioned.

From the moment we sent in our pre-application to the day Akila was placed in our arms, the process took nine months. It was as if the universe was giving us our own symbolic pregnancy, preparing us for the incredible responsibility of parenthood. Akila was born on August 5, but the day we brought her home—September 9—became the date etched into our hearts forever.

Years later, we would come to realize that September 9 carried even more significance than we had initially understood. That day in 1999 was the inaugural International Fetal Alcohol Spectrum Disorder Awareness Day—9/9/99, a date chosen to represent the nine months of pregnancy and the importance of abstaining from alcohol during that time. It was a connection we wouldn't fully grasp until six years later, but looking back, it feels as though fate was gently weaving our story together all along.

Adjusting to parenthood

Those first few months with Akila were a whirlwind of joy, sleepless nights, and a steep learning curve. Michael and I weren't strangers to children—we had spent years babysitting nieces, nephews, and the children of close friends. Michael, an accountant by profession, is surprisingly playful and has always had an incredible way with kids. He's the kind of person children instinctively trust, as they are drawn to his gentle demeanor and infectious humor.

I, on the other hand, had always been more comfortable working with teenagers. For years, I had been a youth worker, helping teens navigate the often messy waters of adolescence. I loved their honesty, their resilience, and even their rebellious streaks. Little kids, on the other hand, were a different story. I liked them—of course I did—but I often found their boundless energy and unpredictability overwhelming, especially in groups.

When I worked in community education for Bloomington Public Schools in Minnesota, I was the sole staff member in the Youth and Family Department who worked with teenagers. The other 11 coordinators worked with elementary-aged children, and I was often asked to help out during summer programming when all ages were consolidated into one building. I dreaded those days. While my colleagues thrived with the younger kids, I felt like a fish out of water. I preferred teenagers, and my favorite ones were the ones who would tell me to "f*ck off." Years later, when I was actually living with teenagers who said that to me, I no longer enjoyed it.

The early days with Akila

During her first year of life, Akila hit most of her developmental milestones right on schedule. She rolled over, babbled, and eventually walked and talked just as the parenting books said she should. But even in those early days, there were hints that her journey might not be entirely typical.

Her sleep patterns were erratic, to say the least. Nights were often punctuated by crying fits and restless tossing. We vividly remember her zoning out at times, staring at the ceiling with an intensity that made Michael uneasy. While I brushed it off as one of her quirks, Michael worried there might be more to it.

When Akila began walking and talking, her energy seemed to multiply overnight. She was a whirlwind, constantly on the move, with a sense of curiosity that kept us on our toes. At one point, I tried to express my concerns to her pediatrician. I wondered aloud if her energy levels might be unusual or if her behavior was indicative of something more. The doctor dismissed my worries, reassuring me that Akila was perfectly normal. She told me to purchase the book *The Spirited Child*, and suggested I give it a read. I did—and promptly donated it to a thrift store. The book didn't offer any solutions for the challenges we were facing.

Akila's energy was both her greatest gift and our greatest challenge. She was funny, engaging, and endlessly curious, but she was also exhausting. I often joke that she never truly sat still. By the time she was two and a half years old, she had mastered the art of cheeky comebacks. If I asked her to do something, she'd look me straight in the eye and say, "I'm busy now," before darting off to her next adventure.

One summer afternoon, I had a moment that encapsulated both the joy and the terror of parenting Akila. We were sitting together on our second-floor deck, enjoying the sunshine. I turned away for what felt like a second, and when I looked back, Akila had squeezed through the railing and was standing on the ledge. My heart stopped. Michael, who was mowing the lawn below, saw the entire scene unfold. Thankfully, we managed to get her back to safety without incident, but the memory still sends shivers down my spine.

Growing our family

When Akila was one year old, we adopted our second child, Imani. From the start, Imani had a completely different temperament. She was calm, easy going, and content to observe the world around her. In contrast, Akila's high-energy personality seemed amplified by the arrival of her younger sibling.

Akila adored Imani but often expressed her love in ways that were, shall we say, overwhelming. She would poke Imani's eyes, steal her blanket or pacifier, and even pull the bottle out of her mouth mid-feeding. It wasn't malicious—Akila simply didn't have an "off" switch when it came to her interactions. Over the next two years, our family grew even more. First, we adopted Hezekiah, and a year later, Ezekiel—whom we affectionately call Zeke—joined our clan. Zeke's arrival brought new challenges. Born prematurely, he came home on oxygen, an apnea monitor, and a list of medications that felt daunting at first. His first six months were marked by a series of hospitalizations, each one more terrifying than the last. It was a very intense time as we had four children under the age of four.

One evening after adopting Zeke, we discovered that he wasn't breathing well. I called our clinic's nurse line, and they advised me to go to the emergency department. Although Hezekiah had been hospitalized at our local hospital a few months prior with breathing issues (he was eventually diagnosed with asthma), I decided to take Zeke to the Children's Hospital of Minnesota after seeing their TV commercials. The care we received there was incredible. Zeke was admitted and hospitalized for weeks several times over the course of his first six months.

Looking for answers: Connecting the dots

During one of Zeke's hospital stays, I realized that the Children's Hospital was not just a hospital—it was part of the larger network known as Children's Hospital and Clinics of Minnesota. As we spent more time there with Zeke as an inpatient, I got to know some of the nurses well. They were a lifeline during some of our most challenging moments, offering not just medical care but emotional support too. One day, during a casual conversation, a nurse mentioned their general pediatric clinic.

At the time, we had been seeing the same pediatrician for three and a half years. While our pediatrician was competent, I had started to feel that our concerns—especially about Akila—weren't being taken seriously. The Children's Hospital, on the other hand, had already impressed me with its comprehensive and compassionate approach. When one of the nurses added a note to Zeke's chart suggesting a pediatrician stop by to meet us, I felt a glimmer of hope.

The next day, Dr. Paula Mackey, one of the pediatricians at the Children's Hospital, stopped by to meet Zeke and me. From the moment she introduced herself, I felt an instant connection. Dr. Mackey asked thoughtful questions about Zeke's health, but what stood out was the way she genuinely listened. She didn't rush through the conversation or dismiss my concerns. Her empathy and curiosity set her apart.

Right then and there, I made a decision: I was switching all four of our kids to Dr. Mackey. It turned out to be one of the smartest parenting decisions I've ever made.

A new approach to care

A month or two after Zeke's health stabilized, I brought Akila, Imani, Hezekiah, and Zeke in for an appointment at the clinic. Let me paint a picture of that day: I had a double stroller loaded with all four of my children–aged three, two, and one, and a newborn. Zeke was still on oxygen and an apnea monitor, and Akila was her usual high-energy self. I think the clinic staff braced themselves whenever they saw us coming. They would often call the Child Life department for extra support, and a specialist would help us navigate the appointment. This was one of the many things I appreciated about Children's—they didn't just tolerate our chaos, they accommodated it.

As we made our way to the exam room that day, I saw Dr. Mackey wave at us from down the hall. When Dr. Mackey entered the room, she immediately honed in on something I hadn't even mentioned: Akila's gait. "Is she pigeon-toed?" she asked. Surprised, I replied, "No, but she does walk on her toes all the time." Dr. Mackey nodded thoughtfully and made a note in the chart. She explained that persistent toe-walking beyond age two could indicate neurological concerns and recommended a neurology consult. She also pointed out other subtle signs—Akila's small head circumference, her being under the fifth percentile for height and weight, and her high muscle tone—all of which warranted further evaluation.

What struck me most about this interaction was how proactive Dr. Mackey was. These were all concerns I had raised with our previous pediatrician, only to be dismissed as an over-anxious mom. I hadn't even mentioned them to Dr. Mackey yet, and she picked up on them immediately. It was a stark reminder of the difference a skilled and attentive provider can make.

The neurology consult

Several months later, we met with a neurologist who conducted a thorough exam and reviewed Akila's history. He noted her small stature and head size, suggesting that these could be linked to prenatal alcohol exposure. While he didn't dwell on the possibility, the comment lingered in my mind. To rule out other potential causes, he ordered a chromosomal analysis.

The results came back a few months later, revealing that Akila had Turner syndrome. Specifically, she was diagnosed with Mosaic Turner syndrome, a form of the condition where some but not all cells are missing the second X chromosome.

Understanding Turner syndrome

Turner syndrome is a chromosomal abnormality that exclusively affects girls. It often leads to short stature, infertility, and a range of medical and developmental challenges, including cardiovascular issues, autoimmune disorders, and learning disabilities. Many girls with Turner syndrome are also at an increased risk for attention deficit hyperactivity disorder (ADHD) and related executive functioning difficulties. While no diagnosis is ever "welcome," this one provided some answers. It explained several of Akila's physical traits, including her small stature and head circumference, as well as some of her developmental and behavioral challenges.

Armed with this new diagnosis, Michael and I immersed ourselves in learning everything we could about Turner syndrome. We booked appointments with specialists in cardiology, endocrinology, ophthalmology, and other fields to ensure Akila received comprehensive care. It felt overwhelming at times, but having a clearer understanding of her needs made it easier to advocate for her.

The IEP and early school years

When Akila was three and a half years old, I took her for the preschool screening required by Minnesota. She passed the screening with flying colors, but there was one notable comment in the report: "Significant behaviors per mother's report." Despite the challenges I described, she was deemed developmentally on track. We were able to secure an Individualized Education Program (IEP) for her based on her Turner syndrome diagnosis a few years later when she was starting kindergarten.

Looking back, the Turner syndrome diagnosis was a blessing in disguise. It served as a key that unlocked resources and support for Akila. Without it, we would have had to fight tooth and nail to secure an IEP—an all-too-common struggle for many families. The IEP provided accommodations that helped Akila navigate school, where her high energy and impulsivity were noticeable but not yet extreme. At home, however, the challenges were a different story.

Reflections on Turner syndrome

Turner syndrome brought clarity to some aspects of Akila's development, but it didn't explain everything. As the years went on, her behaviors intensified in ways that couldn't be fully attributed to Turner syndrome alone. She remained stuck in what felt like an extended toddler tantrum phase, with meltdowns and impulsivity that disrupted daily life. While the diagnosis opened doors to support, it also raised more questions.

This period marked the beginning of our journey to uncover the full picture of Akila's needs. It was a winding road filled with trial and error, but it also taught us the importance of persistence, advocacy, and finding the right professionals who truly listen. Dr. Mackey's attention to detail and willingness to dig deeper set us on a path that would eventually lead to greater understanding—not just of Akila's conditions but also of how to meet her where she was.

The Turner syndrome diagnosis was a critical piece of the puzzle, but as we would later learn, it was only one part of a much larger story.

Addressing the stealing behaviors

The first time Akila stole was at two years old in our church nursery. She tried to hide toys in her pockets when we picked her up. This is typical toddler behavior, as they don't understand the abstract concept of ownership. Akila, however, didn't learn not to steal after being given consequences, and the behavior continued.

Some individuals with fetal alcohol spectrum disorder (FASD) never grasp the concept of ownership, or it takes many years. The toddler rules of ownership seem to persist:

- If I like it, it's mine.
- If it's in my hand, it's mine.
- If I can take it from you, it's mine.
- If I had it a little while ago, it's mine.
- If it's mine, it must never appear to be yours in any way.

- If I'm building something, all the pieces are mine.
- If it looks just like mine, it is mine.
- If I saw it first, it's mine.
- If you play with something and put it down, it automatically becomes mine.

Eventually, Akila did grasp the concept of ownership—but the stealing continued. It became one of the most perplexing and frustrating challenges we faced as a family in these early years. What made it even more confusing was the nature of the items she took. Akila didn't steal from stores or strangers. Instead, her targets were often places of trust: family gatherings, church, friends' homes, and, most frequently, our own house. It wasn't just about missing items—it was about the constant uncertainty of what might go missing next. Our home felt less like a sanctuary and more like a treasure hunt for misplaced objects.

Attempts to curb the behavior

We tried everything we could think of to address the behavior. Consequences became our go-to approach. We took away her toys, denied her treats, canceled activities, and revoked playdates. These punishments ranged from a single day to an entire week, depending on the severity of the situation. None of it worked. Akila remained unfazed, as though the punishments were happening to someone else entirely. The disconnect between action and consequence became glaringly apparent, but at the time, we didn't understand why.

Desperate for support, we sought help from therapists. They offered token economy systems—behavior charts, points, rewards, and other external motivators. At first, these systems seemed promising, giving us a renewed sense of hope. But it didn't take long to realize their limitations. (I'll explain more about why token systems often fail children with FASD, in Chapter 6.) Akila's behaviors remained unaffected by these efforts, leaving us feeling more helpless than before.

We turned to positive reinforcement, another widely recommended strategy. We praised her for good behavior, trying to catch her in the act of doing something right. We structured her days with rigid schedules and consistent rules. There was even a three-month period where we doubled down, deciding to enforce consequences for every little misstep, no matter how minor. It was exhausting, emotionally draining, and completely ineffective. Instead of improving, Akila's behavior escalated, and the atmosphere in our home grew increasingly toxic.

We also experimented with social stories, crafting narratives to help Akila understand the social implications of stealing and other behaviors. These stories were carefully designed to resonate with children and provide teachable moments. But for Akila, they didn't click. It was as if we were speaking a different language. The strategies felt like Band-Aids on a wound we didn't fully understand.

Tracking the patterns

By the time Akila was six years old and in first grade, we were still no closer to a solution. Therapists recommended we start tracking her stealing to identify patterns or triggers. Eager for answers, we began meticulously documenting every incident. We noted when and where it happened, what she stole, and any surrounding circumstances.

At first, the data seemed to reveal some patterns. For example, there were periods when Akila stole daily for weeks, followed by stretches where she didn't take anything. But the more we tracked, the less sense it made. The patterns were inconsistent, and potential triggers were elusive. Some days, she stole after school, while other times, she took items during a family gathering or seemingly at random. It was like trying to solve a puzzle with pieces that didn't fit.

The things Akila stole were baffling. Often, they were duplicates of items she already owned—a pencil identical to one in her desk, a doll that matched one in her toybox, or a pair of mittens identical to her own. Other times, they were completely random, like a decorative paperweight from a neighbor's house or a half-used eraser from a classmate's desk. The act of stealing seemed to be the goal, not the possession itself.

Conversations and lectures

Each time we caught Akila stealing, we sat her down for a talk. We explained, in painstaking detail, why stealing was wrong. We discussed how it made people feel, the importance of respecting others' belongings, and the need to earn trust. These lectures often turned into long-winded monologues, with us repeating the same points over and over, hoping something would stick.

When reasoning didn't work, we turned to shaming. We told her she was breaking our trust and reminded her that "nobody likes a liar." Looking back, it's painful to remember the words we used. At the time, we were desperate and overwhelmed, but in hindsight, we were only adding to Akila's shame and confusion. The stealing continued, unimpeded by our efforts.

A desperate attempt to solve the problem

One evening, after yet another incident when Akila was six years old, Michael and I had a heart-to-heart about Akila's stealing. The calls from school, family, and neighbors were piling up, and we felt like failures as parents. We thought we needed to take drastic action to regain control.

We went into parenting with a lot of confidence—too much confidence, if we're honest. We had years of babysitting experience with nieces, nephews, and friends' kids. I even babysat for a friend twice a week for years, with Michael helping regularly.

We thought we were seasoned pros. Worse, we were judgmental. Watching friends and family navigate parenthood, we critiqued their choices, silently vowing never to make the same "mistakes." Oh, how clueless we were. Looking back, I cringe at our arrogance and owe those parents an apology.

In our misguided determination, we decided to "go big or go home." We asked ourselves, "What is the most important possession Akila owns?" The answer was clear: her yellow blankie. That blanket was her lifeline. It went everywhere with her, providing comfort and security. We thought, surely, if we made the stakes high enough, she'd stop stealing.

So we laid down the law. One evening, we sat Akila down and told her, "Stealing is not acceptable in this family. If you steal again, we will throw your blankie away—forever." We emphasized the word "forever," ensuring she understood the gravity of the consequence. She nodded solemnly, clutching her blanket tightly, and promised not to steal again. We were convinced this was the breakthrough we had been waiting for.

The blanket debacle

The very next day, Akila came home from school—and she had stolen again. I don't even remember what the item was that day, but I remember the devastation we felt. We had made a promise, and now we had to follow through.

That evening, we gathered all four kids in the alley behind our house. We explained to Akila why stealing was unacceptable and reiterated the importance of trust. Then, we made her throw her blanket into the trash can. I even slammed the lid shut for dramatic effect, hoping the moment would leave a lasting impression. Akila was crying, as were all of the other kids.

That night was rough. Akila didn't sleep—how could she? We had just taken away her most treasured possession, her sensory anchor. At the time, we didn't understand sensory processing disorders or how crucial that blanket was for her regulation. We chalked her sleeplessness up to defiance and resolved to stay firm.

The next day, she came home from school—and she had stolen again. This time, it was a ten-dollar bill. It was the first time she had stolen money, and I was livid. Desperate for help, I drove straight to her school to speak with the school psychologist we'd been working with. I laid out everything we had tried, including the story of the blanket. Her response? "We don't usually see this unless the child is in a homeless shelter or foster care. I don't know what to tell you." That was it—no solutions, no guidance. I left feeling defeated.

A light bulb moment

That night, after the kids went to bed, I stayed up late, frantically searching the internet for answers. I typed in phrases like "childhood theft" and "kids stealing." That's when I stumbled on a website about fetal alcohol spectrum disorder. I remember the moment vividly: the layout of the website, the colors, the text—everything. As I read through the common symptoms, it was as if a light bulb went on. Akila had nearly every one of them.

We had always known Akila was exposed to alcohol prenatally—it was in her case file. But because she didn't have the telltale facial features associated with fetal alcohol syndrome and was bright, we had never considered it a factor. My education in youth development had left me with a narrow understanding of FASD. I thought it only applied to children who looked visibly disabled and had low cognitive abilities. Akila didn't fit that profile, but suddenly, everything started to make sense.

That night marked the beginning of a new journey—a journey of understanding, growth, and learning to parent Akila in a way that honored her unique brain. It also marked the start of a transformation in our family, as we began to unlearn everything we thought we knew about parenting and embrace a more compassionate, informed approach.

Stop the blame game

Before I move on, I need to address the elephant in the room. Yes, Akila's first mom (some say birth mom) used alcohol while pregnant. Many of you may be judging her and feeling anger toward her for doing that to this precious girl. I'm not going to lie: I went through a stage of being angry too. But after I learned more about FASD and substance use disorders (SUDs), I let go of that anger and blame.

She did not do this on purpose—no parent ever does. She struggled with substance use disorders from her early teen years, and I suspect she may have FASD herself, as her case file notes that both of her parents also struggled with SUD. In my view, there are three main scenarios in which a parent might prenatally expose their child to alcohol:

1. If they are struggling with substance use disorder.
2. If they had an unplanned pregnancy (about 45% of pregnancies in the U.S. and U.K. are unplanned).
3. If they had been misinformed that light or moderate drinking during pregnancy is acceptable.

With so many pregnancies being unplanned, combined with high rates of alcohol use, millions of people are likely walking around with undiagnosed FASD. Many of them were probably misdiagnosed with ADHD, bipolar disorder, conduct disorder, reactive attachment disorder, or other conditions.

There are still professionals, including medical doctors, who tell people it is okay to use alcohol lightly or moderately during pregnancy. Many of us caregivers sometimes joke that they should take our kids for a week and see if they change their minds. Globally, most doctors only know about and can recognize fetal alcohol syndrome (FAS), where the child has facial features, growth deficits, and cognitive challenges. However, it has been established in research for years that most individuals on the fetal alcohol spectrum do not have the facial features of FAS, and the majority have IQs well above 70. Some individuals with FASD even have high IQs, though most fall into the average or low-average range. *This is a really important fact. Less than 10% of the children on the fetal alcohol spectrum have the facial features of fetal alcohol syndrome.*[1]

Several years ago, there was an economist who wrote a book claiming that it's okay to drink one glass of alcohol per day during pregnancy. Naturally, our FASD community was upset. This is dangerous and irresponsible. I believe that FASD is the number one public health epidemic, though society has not woken up to it. I believe FASD is the root cause behind many of the public health crises we focus on—substance use disorders, mental health issues, community violence, teenage pregnancy, the list goes on. A large percentage of those affected by these issues likely have undiagnosed or diagnosed FASD. Yet, the interventions and strategies being implemented to address these issues often fail to recognize or accommodate this hidden brain injury.

My own prenatal exposure

During the editing process of this book, I went in for FASD diagnostics for myself and I was diagnosed on the fetal alcohol spectrum. I was born in the 1960s, before FASD was discovered in the United States (it was first identified in 1973 in Washington state). Prior to this, doctors often recommended that women drink alcohol during pregnancy. It was thought to calm nerves or help the baby drop.

When a woman went into premature labor, they would even use alcohol drips in IVs to stop contractions.

When I worked as a Family Resource Coordinator at Proof Alliance, a Minnesota-based FASD advocacy organization, I met two families who realized that their adult children in their forties had FASD from receiving alcohol drips in the hospital during pregnancy. Imagine how many hundreds of thousands of adults have undiagnosed FASD because of this, and how mind-blowing that number is! I wish we could gather these adults and their families to go public with their stories—it would be incredibly powerful.

My mother used alcohol socially on the weekends while pregnant with me. We were just beginning to suspect Akila had FASD when my mother passed away from cancer. I remember her not understanding FASD because, as she said, "I drank while pregnant with you, and you're fine." What neither of us knew at the time was just how broad the FASD spectrum is.

In Chapter 4, I talk about common symptoms, one of which is that many individuals with FASD struggle with math. Math has always been difficult for me—I've always had an intense hatred for anything math-related, which meant I hated science, economics, and any subject involving numbers. In high school, I was always placed in basic or lower-level math classes, and I barely passed them. I changed my major several times in college just to avoid math, and eventually created my own degree at the University of Minnesota to bypass math and economics. It was a relatively new degree program called the Bachelor of Individualized Studies, where you chose three major areas and wrote a proposal for an individualized degree. It was the perfect option for me.

I am a night owl and have always struggled with sleep and I also have ADHD. I have sensory processing issues as well and difficulty with brain functions like "crossing the midline", which refers to the ability to move a limb or body part across the imaginary center line of the body. For instance, in a step aerobics class, I can handle basic moves like stepping up and down or the A-step. The A-step is a foundational move in step aerobics where you step up onto the platform with one foot, then bring the other foot up to meet it, and step back down with the first foot followed by the second. But when we're asked to cross over the step or do fancy footwork, my brain freezes. Knitting or crocheting doesn't work for me either. Years ago, a personal care attendant (PCA) was teaching Akila to knit, and after the PCA left, Akila wanted to continue. I tried watching a YouTube video about knitting 20 times, but I still couldn't figure it out. If I loved knitting, I'd be willing to work hard on it, but I'm not a crafty person. Oddly enough, Akila has started crocheting in the past year and is very gifted at it.

Am I mad at my mother for using alcohol during pregnancy? Of course not. She wouldn't have done it if she had known it could impact me. The effects of her social drinking weren't severe, but they did make some things more challenging for me. What I often tell people is that it's just not worth the risk—it can take away potential. There are so many factors that determine the level of damage a developing fetus might experience. I will cover this in the next chapter.

In the spring of 2005, Akila was diagnosed with alcohol-related neurodevelopmental disorder (ARND), a type of fetal alcohol spectrum disorder. It is a "hidden" diagnosis, meaning it isn't visible from the outside. The diagnosis started us on a new journey—a journey filled with many highs and lows. This book will share with you some of those experiences.

I'm naturally an optimistic person, but I also like to learn from my mistakes, and I've made many. I often say that most of my training and coaching came from learning through failures and trying to help other caregivers and professionals avoid the same mistakes. This is why I'm writing this book. If just one of you is able to avoid some of the mistakes I made and can say this book made your life a little easier, then the frustration I'm feeling as I write it will have been worth it. (I like to talk—I don't like to write.)

Chapter 2

FASD Unpacked: Understanding the Basics

FASD: More than just fetal alcohol syndrome

Many people have heard of fetal alcohol syndrome (FAS), but few realize it's part of a broader spectrum called fetal alcohol spectrum disorder (FASD). The impact of prenatal alcohol exposure varies widely, depending on timing, amount, frequency of alcohol use, and other factors. FASD reflects this complexity, as no two individuals are affected in exactly the same way.

Pregnancy, divided into three trimesters, is a critical period lasting approximately 40 weeks. There is no safe trimester for alcohol use. The first trimester poses the highest risk, as this is when vital organs and systems are forming, making the developing fetus particularly vulnerable to harm. However, alcohol exposure at any stage can have lasting and serious effects.

During my deep dive into understanding FASD, I served on several committees at Children's Hospital and Clinics of Minnesota, now known as "Children's Minnesota", including Education & Research, Health Care Home, and the Family Advisory Committee. At a statewide conference with my Health Care Home team, I encountered a troubling misconception. A pregnant pediatrician in her thirties shared that some of her friends—a teacher, a doctor, and a lawyer—had argued it was safe to drink alcohol during the third trimester because the baby is "fully developed and just growing larger." One friend even cited an article supporting this view.

This myth is dangerously misleading. Although a baby's physical development is nearing completion in the third trimester, the brain is still actively growing and forming critical neural connections. Alcohol exposure during this time can cause significant damage, reducing the child's potential and leading to lifelong challenges.

I've gained valuable insights about FASD from Dr. Ira Chasnoff's webinars and books. In a 2021 webinar I participated in, Dr. Chasnoff explained that alcohol exposure during the third trimester is particularly likely to impact the child's IQ.

The potential harm from prenatal alcohol exposure far outweighs any perceived benefits. Choosing to avoid alcohol entirely during pregnancy is the safest and best way to protect the child's health and potential.

The cost of a missed diagnosis

During my time working at Proof Alliance, I met a couple raising a nine-year-old son who had been prenatally exposed to alcohol. Their story is one I hear all too often, and it underscores the devastating impact of a missed diagnosis.

Ten years earlier, the mother had been a university student who discovered she was unexpectedly pregnant at ten weeks. At the time, she had been binge drinking—a behavior quite common in college settings. Concerned about the impact on her baby, she visited an obstetric-gynecologist who advised her to stop drinking immediately, as should always be the recommendation. Wanting reassurance, she was referred to a geneticist for further testing. All the tests came back normal, and her son was born with a healthy birth weight and high Apgar scores (a quick assessment of a newborn's health status conducted at one minute and five minutes after birth).

In his early years, the boy seemed to develop on track, although he exhibited challenging behaviors as a toddler. His mother, now married, had two subsequent children who were not prenatally exposed. The couple were devoted parents with a strong support network. Despite their best efforts, by the time their son entered elementary school, his behaviors became increasingly difficult to manage.

He received multiple clinical interventions and was eventually diagnosed with ADHD and conduct disorder. Throughout this process, the parents consistently reported the prenatal alcohol exposure. Yet, for nine years, their concerns were dismissed by multiple professionals because their son didn't have the facial features associated with FAS.

At nine years old, after his behaviors escalated to the point of requiring a residential treatment center, the family finally encountered a professional who understood FASD. The boy was referred to an FASD diagnostic clinic, where he was diagnosed with alcohol-related neurodevelopmental disorder, a condition on the FASD spectrum. By then, the family was in crisis, a situation I see far too often in the FASD community.

The missed diagnosis had taken an immeasurable toll on the family. The parents' marriage was strained to the point of divorce eventually, their son's relationship with his parents and siblings was fractured, and his self-esteem had plummeted. He struggled in school, and the relationship between the family and the school had become adversarial.

For nine years, the family used strategies that were ineffective for a brain injury like FASD. This not only cost them thousands of dollars from their own pocket and through insurance, but also exacted a heavy emotional toll. The right diagnosis early on could have profoundly changed their journey. With proper understanding and interventions, they could have mitigated much of the pain, frustration, and heartbreak they endured.

This story is a powerful reminder of why early identification and intervention are so crucial for individuals with FASD. Recognizing and addressing the brain-based challenges early can significantly improve outcomes—not just for the individual but for the entire family. When FASD goes unrecognized or misunderstood, the costs are often devastating, both financially and emotionally.

What factors cause damage to a fetus?

Genetics play a significant role in determining the extent of damage a fetus may experience from alcohol exposure. Research on twins has shown that identical twins, who share the same genetic makeup, are impacted in similar ways by the same prenatal alcohol exposure. In contrast, fraternal twins, who have different genetic compositions, often show vastly different outcomes from the same exposure. This highlights that a fetus's genetic makeup is a critical factor in how alcohol affects their development.[1]

A pregnant person's metabolism also influences how alcohol impacts the fetus. Even among two individuals of the same age, weight, and gender who drink the same amount of alcohol at the same pace, blood alcohol concentration levels will vary. Similarly, the fetus and the pregnant person metabolize alcohol differently.

For a significant portion of pregnancy, the fetus lacks fully developed internal organs capable of processing alcohol efficiently. Additionally, the amniotic fluid acts as a reservoir, prolonging the fetus's exposure to alcohol even after the parent has metabolized it. This extended exposure is due to the fetus's constant need for nutrients, which surpasses the parent's intake. It's why small, frequent meals are recommended during pregnancy.

The pregnant person's nutrition plays a crucial role in mitigating the severity of alcohol exposure. Research shows that higher levels of nutrients such as iron, folic acid, choline, betaine, and vitamin B12 in the parent can reduce the damage caused by alcohol to the fetus.[2] Proper nutrition acts as a protective factor, creating a buffer against some of the harm.

In my own case, I benefited from my mother's excellent nutrition during her pregnancy. She maintained a well-balanced diet and didn't face significant stressors like economic hardship, domestic violence, or mental health challenges. That said, raising two older brothers—especially my brother Tony—probably gave her enough stress to keep her hands full (love you Tony, but you know you were a handful!). Still, her strong nutrition and overall stability likely mitigated the impact of my prenatal alcohol exposure.

The role of stress during pregnancy

Stress is an unavoidable part of life, and every pregnant parent will experience it to some degree. However, *toxic stress*—stress that is consistent, prolonged, and occurs at high levels—can have significant effects on a developing fetus.

When a person is stressed, their body produces cortisol, a stress hormone. Research has shown that high levels of cortisol during pregnancy can impact fetal development. For example, children born to parents with elevated cortisol levels throughout pregnancy are more likely to experience depressive symptoms in adolescence. These children also tend to have less cortical thickness in their brains, which is associated with cognitive impairments and an increased risk of depression.[3]

Additionally, research has linked high levels of stress during pregnancy to an increased likelihood of ADHD in children. This highlights the importance of addressing and managing stress during pregnancy, as it can have long-term effects on a child's mental health and development.[4] Many children who have FASD also receive the double whammy of being exposed to high amounts of cortisol during pregnancy.

In my own life, I benefited from the fact that my mother's stress during pregnancy was not toxic. She experienced the typical day-to-day stress that most people encounter, but it wasn't prolonged or at the extreme levels associated with toxic stress. This likely served as a protective factor for me, mitigating the potential impact of prenatal alcohol exposure.

The link between stress and behavioral issues in foster, adoption, and kinship care

The connection between prenatal stress and behavioral challenges is indeed profound, particularly in the context of adoption, foster care, and kinship care. These systems often serve children who have faced significant adversities even before birth, stemming from the chronic stressors their first parents experienced. Understanding this connection is essential for developing more effective support strategies for these children and their caregivers.

Key considerations for behavioral issues in these populations

- **Prenatal stress and cortisol exposure:** Chronic stress during pregnancy elevates cortisol levels, which can disrupt fetal brain development.

- **Intersection with FASD:** Many first parents of children in foster, adoption, or kinship care may unknowingly have

FASD themselves, influencing their decision-making, coping abilities, and parenting practices.

- These parents may struggle with managing their stress, leading to heightened cortisol exposure for their unborn child. For children with prenatal alcohol exposure and stress exposure, the neurodevelopmental impacts are often compounded.

- **Environmental and postnatal challenges:** Postnatal experiences such as multiple placements, disrupted attachments, or inconsistent caregiving can exacerbate behavioral issues rooted in prenatal exposures. A child's sense of safety and stability plays a crucial role in mitigating these challenges.

- **Strengthening caregiver understanding:**
  - Caregivers in foster, adoption, and kinship care often encounter behaviors they do not immediately understand. Providing training on how prenatal stress, trauma, and conditions like FASD shape behavior can empower caregivers to respond with empathy and effective strategies.
  - Recognizing the potential for prenatal factors helps shift the narrative from "bad behavior" to "adaptive survival responses," which can transform how children are supported.

FASD can look like autism or ADHD

The current prevalence of FASD in the United States is 1 in 20 children.[5] This is nearly double the prevalence of autism spectrum disorder (ASD), which affects 1 in 36 children.[6] Many of us who have deeply studied FASD believe its true prevalence is even higher than current research indicates. How many adults, like myself, are walking around affected by FASD without knowing it? How many children currently diagnosed with ADHD, oppositional defiant disorder (ODD), conduct disorder, or other conditions are actually living with an undiagnosed FASD?

We don't know the exact number, but my experiences of supporting families whose children have initially been misdiagnosed with autism when in fact they have FASD leads me to believe that this is a widespread problem. This is not to say autism doesn't exist—it absolutely does. However, in some cases, FASD may be the more accurate diagnosis.

There are two major differences I've observed between autism and FASD:

1. **Communication styles:** Many children with autism whom I have known exhibit quirky communication challenges, such as avoiding eye contact and showing little interest in initiating social interactions, especially with unfamiliar people.

2. **Social behavior:** Children with FASD, in contrast, are often eager to talk to anyone, including strangers, and actively seek out social interactions. Generally, they have good eye contact and communication skills, but they do struggle to read social cues similar to those with autism.

Understanding these differences is crucial for accurate diagnosis and support. Misdiagnosis can result in inappropriate interventions and missed opportunities to address the unique challenges of FASD effectively.

ADHD is another common misdiagnosis for FASD. Children with ADHD and FASD share some similarities, such as difficulties with focus and attention. However, there are key differences that can significantly impact how they learn and retain information.

Imagine two children—one with ADHD and one with FASD—

sitting down to complete some homework. We know it's beneficial to prepare them by letting them expend some energy through a sensory activity, providing a healthy snack, having them jump on a trampoline, and creating a calm environment. Once they're settled, both children are able to focus on the worksheet for 10–15 minutes and comprehend the material. Recognizing their short attention spans, we take a 30-minute break before resuming the task.

What often happens is this: the child with ADHD retains the information and picks up where they left off, while the child with FASD may struggle to recall the material and often needs to start over.

This difference is partly due to the working memory challenges common in individuals with FASD. Working memory is like a mental "sticky note" that helps us hold and manipulate information in the moment. For children with FASD, this sticky note may fail, making it hard for them to retain or apply information.

However, in many cases, the problem isn't that the information wasn't retained; it's that they can't access it when needed. This can make everyday learning feel like the movie *Groundhog Day*, where Bill Murray's character wakes up to the same day over and over again. A key factor in this inconsistency is damage to the corpus callosum, a thick bundle of fibers in the center of the brain that connects the left and right hemispheres. I will cover this more in Chapter 4.

Who loved middle school?

When I train people in person, I often ask the audience to raise their hand if middle school or junior high was their favorite time of childhood (typically grades 6th-8th). Occasionally, one person will raise their hand, but it's rare. Middle school is challenging for most adolescents and especially so for those with FASD. Personally,

I remember feeling immense relief when our youngest finally entered high school, leaving the drama of middle school behind. I also remember how hard junior high was for me.

Many children with FASD do well in preschool and the early elementary years. This is because the curriculum in these early grades aligns with typical child brain development—it is highly concrete, focusing on foundational skills like learning the ABCs and 123s. Tests are simple, such as spelling tests, which don't require higher-level decision-making skills. The curriculum in these years works better for the brains of children with FASD.

For many children with FASD, these early years provide a sense of accomplishment. However, as they progress into fourth grade and beyond, the curriculum becomes more abstract, requiring higher-level brain functions that develop naturally in neurotypical children. For children with FASD, these changes can lead to a significant wall of frustration and struggle.

The increasing complexity of the curriculum, including word problems and multiple-choice tests designed to challenge memory, often exacerbates anxiety. For children with FASD, deficits in working memory and heightened anxiety make these tasks even more difficult, leading to frustration and a decline in academic performance.

This increased anxiety manifests in different ways. Some children feel a constant undercurrent of stress throughout the day, which limits their ability to focus and learn. Others manage to hold it together at school but release their emotions at home, where they feel safer. This phenomenon is often referred to as the *delayed effect*.

Schools frequently tell caregivers that their child is "doing fine" in class and doesn't need the accommodations outlined in their individualized plans—accommodations the caregivers have often fought hard to secure. What educators may not realize is that these accommodations help reduce the student's anxiety, allowing them to function better, not just academically but emotionally as well.

The goal of these supports is not merely academic success but also fostering overall stability and well-being, both in and outside the classroom.

The delayed effect: Behaviors at home

Children with FASD often suppress their emotions during the school day, only to release them at home. While this pattern is common in most children to some extent, the behaviors associated with FASD are often far more intense. These behaviors may include yelling, hitting, kicking, or other forms of dysregulation. For years, my husband and I felt like we were losing our minds. Akila behaved beautifully at school but would rage all evening. School staff often praised her behavior, leaving us questioning what we were doing wrong. I've seen this same scenario unfold for countless families I've worked with.

Eventually, we realized the main reason Akila managed to hold it together at school and in the community but not at home was because she felt safe at home. She spent the entire day at school working hard to keep her anxiety under control, and when she got home—where most of us unwind after a tough day—she truly let go.

Most neurotypical people have the filters to keep it together after a hard day. We might get cranky, short-tempered, or even raise our voices, but we generally don't experience full meltdowns that can become physical.

Medications can also contribute to this pattern. Many children with FASD are prescribed medications that help them function during school hours but begin to wear off by the time they get home. Even families with neurotypical children report that kids are often "worse" for their parents than for others. For children with FASD, this dynamic is typically even more pronounced.

As academic demands increase, children with FASD often begin to feel "dumb" because they struggle to keep up. This challenge is compounded by the developmental profile common in children with FASD, where their functional level is often closer to half their chronological age (this topic will be covered in greater depth in Chapter 6). In early elementary school, these developmental gaps are less noticeable. However, by middle school, the contrast becomes glaring—when a 12-year-old is functioning socially or emotionally at the level of a 6-year-old, the gap is stark.

This is also when many children with FASD begin to experience social isolation. Same-age peers often pull away, and bullying becomes more prevalent during these years. This is especially challenging for children with FASD, as they are naturally social and crave connection.

I refer to this as the *"trifecta" of challenges* that children with FASD face during this period:

1. They struggle academically and feel "dumb."
2. They feel socially isolated and lonely.
3. They are experiencing the hormonal changes of puberty.

This combination creates a perfect storm that can feel overwhelming for both the child and their family.

The need for accommodations and modifications

If adjustments aren't made at home, in school, and in therapeutic settings, the consequences can be severe. Children may develop negative self-talk, engage in self-harm, experience suicidal ideation, or refuse to attend school altogether.

Unfortunately, one of the hallmark symptoms of FASD is the inability to learn from consequences. Now, imagine how this impacts challenges like school refusal. When training school staff, I often pose this question: "How do you think a caregiver can get an adolescent up in the morning when they don't respond to consequences?"

To support children with FASD during these challenging years, we need to make significant accommodations and modifications in academics. It's essential that they feel welcome and capable when they're at school. For example, I never wanted to be in math class—it may as well have been a foreign language for how much sense it made to me. If I had felt like that during the entire school day, I would never have made it through school.

When we fail to adjust our expectations and strategies, we risk losing these children to a cycle of frustration, failure, and disengagement. By understanding their unique needs and providing the right support, we can help them navigate this difficult period and emerge with their confidence and well-being intact.

More statistics

Dr. Ira Chasnoff has conducted extensive research on FASD, particularly among adopted and foster children. His findings reveal that the FASD diagnosis is missed 86.5% of the time in these populations.[7] In the United States, Minnesota stands out as the first—and as of 2024, the only—state requiring all licensed foster parents to receive annual training on FASD. Additionally, Minnesota successfully enacted a statute mandating that every child entering foster care be screened for prenatal alcohol exposure. These statutes are due to the excellent advocacy work that Proof Alliance does in Minnesota.

It's essential to recognize the deep connection between FASD and trauma. FASD itself is a form of trauma—in-utero trauma. Many individuals with FASD are also grappling with generational trauma that may have been passed down from their ancestors.

One fascinating piece of research explored how trauma tied to odors could be inherited across generations.[8] In this study, researchers exposed male mice to the scent of cherry blossoms while administering mild shocks that caused them pain. Two weeks after this trauma, these male mice mated with female mice and produced offspring.

Their pups, having never been exposed to cherry blossoms or the mild shocks, grew into adults. When researchers introduced the scent of cherry blossoms to these adult offspring, the mice became anxious and fearful. Remarkably, these mice were not even conceived when their fathers experienced the trauma. This study underscores how trauma can alter epigenetic structures—how our genes can be influenced by behaviors and environments.

Adoption, foster care, and trauma

Many children prenatally exposed to alcohol end up in foster care or are placed for adoption. Being separated from their first family is, in itself, a form of trauma. While adoption is often glorified in society—portrayed in media, movies, and books as a purely joyful event—it is crucial to acknowledge the loss and trauma adoptees experience. Adoption can bring hope, joy, and positive change, but it often comes with extreme grief and loss.

Not every adoptee struggles with this loss, but many do. The late adoption scholar and activist Reverend Keith C. Griffith profoundly captured this reality: "Adoption loss is the only trauma in the world where the victims are expected by the whole of society to be grateful."

Throughout my children's lives, countless people have said things like, "You're so lucky to have your parents," or "You're so fortunate Barb and Michael adopted you." Imagine how that feels to an adoptee. These comments imply they should feel fortunate for being separated from their first family. Whether the separation was voluntary or involuntary, happened at birth or later in childhood, it still represents a significant loss. For those without any contact or information about their first family, the questions can be endless: *Who were they? What do they look like? Why was I placed for adoption? Why was I removed from my family?*

This narrative needs to change. While adoption has positive aspects, it is vital to validate and respect the loss and trauma it can bring.

Red flags for FASD

Understanding red flags for FASD is crucial, as early identification can lead to more effective interventions. While these signs do not necessarily confirm an FASD diagnosis, they are indicators that further evaluation might be warranted.

Behavioral and cognitive red flags

- **Doesn't learn from consequences or punishments:** Children with FASD often struggle to connect actions with outcomes. They may repeatedly make the same mistakes despite consistent discipline. This is not typical behavior and points to a neuro-disconnect.

- **Difficulty following rules they know:** If a child can articulate the rules but breaks them minutes later and doesn't understand why they're in trouble, this indicates a breakdown in executive functioning.

- **Actions that don't match their perceived intelligence:** A child who appears bright and articulate but consistently makes choices that seem irrational or unsafe may have challenges with impulse control and processing cause and effect.

- **Big fantastical stories:** Frequent storytelling with unrealistic or fantastical elements could be a sign of confabulation, a memory issue often seen in FASD (see Chapter 8).

- **Emotional dysregulation:** Many children with FASD have a very hard time regulating their emotions. They may easily cry or have verbal or physical explosiveness. Their behaviors can be similar to a toddler tantrum, way beyond their toddler years.

- **Multiple diagnoses that don't fully fit:** If a child has been diagnosed with ADHD, oppositional defiant disorder (ODD), reactive attachment disorder (RAD), autism, or other conditions but these labels don't seem to explain all of their challenges, it's worth considering FASD as an underlying cause.

Biological and familial red flags

- **Family history of substance use disorders:** A first parent with a history of substance use disorders is a significant risk factor for FASD.

- **Eating and sleeping challenges:** Persistent issues with eating (overeating, food hoarding, picky eating, or refusal) or sleeping (difficulty falling or staying asleep) are common in children with FASD. Toileting issues may persist beyond toddler/preschool years.

I jokingly say that numerous Facebook profiles are also a red flag.

This can be due to the fact that they cannot remember passwords or how to get into certain accounts or emails. My daughter has at least five profiles that I am aware of.

These red flags don't confirm an FASD diagnosis, but they can provide caregivers and professionals with important clues. If several of these signs are present, it's worth seeking an evaluation with a professional familiar with FASD.

Early identification is critical. It can pave the way for understanding, tailored supports, and a better quality of life for both the individual and their caregivers.

Diagnosis

Diagnosing FASD is a complex process that varies across countries, diagnostic frameworks, and available resources. As research continues to evolve, our understanding of FASD deepens, leading to changes in diagnostic criteria and the terminology used to describe symptom profiles. This means that a diagnosis given at one time may later be reclassified or renamed under a new diagnostic model.

Given the complexities of diagnostics and the ever-changing nature of this field, I won't focus on specific diagnostic terms in this discussion.

The role of confirmed prenatal alcohol exposure

One of the most challenging aspects of diagnosing FASD is obtaining documented confirmation of prenatal alcohol exposure. For the FASD diagnosis, this confirmation may not always be required if the individual meets all the physical criteria (e.g. facial features) and cognitive profiles. However, for other diagnoses, like alcohol-related neurodevelopmental disorder (ARND) or neurobehavioral disorder associated with prenatal alcohol exposure (ND-PAE), confirmation of prenatal alcohol exposure is essential.

This requirement often creates a barrier to diagnosis, particularly for individuals in foster care, adoption, or other situations where prenatal history may be unknown or undocumented. Without clear evidence, many individuals with FASD may go undiagnosed or misdiagnosed with conditions such as ADHD, autism spectrum disorder, or oppositional defiant disorder.

I have worked with many families where caregivers felt certain their child had FASD but couldn't get a diagnosis due to a lack of documented prenatal alcohol exposure. Often, these children had other diagnoses instead. What I tell these families is to learn about FASD and try the strategies outlined in this book.

You can also inform your child's school team and therapists that you strongly suspect FASD and encourage them to learn about it and use the same strategies.

Why diagnosis matters

Accurate diagnosis is crucial because it provides a framework for understanding the individual's strengths and challenges. It can guide appropriate interventions, accommodations, and access to services. However, due to the complexity of FASD and the stigma surrounding prenatal alcohol use, many individuals remain undiagnosed or receive a diagnosis later in life, often after years of misdiagnosis and ineffective interventions.

A diagnosis not only helps the individual but also empowers caregivers and professionals with the knowledge needed to provide more effective support. As challenging as the process can be, early and accurate diagnosis is a critical first step toward improving outcomes for individuals with FASD.

How to ask

Many of the adoptive and foster families I've worked with over the years strongly suspect their child has FASD but struggle to obtain a diagnosis because they cannot confirm prenatal alcohol exposure.

When I train social workers, I emphasize the importance of investigating this as soon as a child enters the system. Often, adoption paperwork includes missed opportunities, where social workers skimmed through or didn't press harder for critical medical history from the first parents.

When there's an opportunity to speak with a first parent about potential alcohol exposure, I advise against directly asking if they drank alcohol while pregnant. This is a highly loaded question, and many people will instinctively say no to avoid judgment—even if the truthful answer is yes. Instead, I recommend framing the question in a way that feels less shaming.

For example: "Is there any chance you might have been using alcohol before you knew you were pregnant? That has happened to so many of my friends and family." (It has by the way!)

This phrasing reduces judgment and creates space for honesty. In my experience, asking the question this way significantly increases the likelihood of getting accurate information. Numerous families have reached out to me after attending my training to share how this approach helped them finally get the confirmation they needed.

One caregiver told me she had asked her child's first mother about alcohol exposure for years and always received a no—until she rephrased the question as I suggested. For the first time, the mother opened up and provided the needed confirmation.

A message to biological families

If you're reading this book as a biological family, know that I see you, I respect you, and your needs matter. While much of this book focuses on adoptive, foster, and kinship families—because of the high rates of FASD diagnoses in these groups—I also recognize the unique dynamics biological families face.

One dynamic I've observed in working with biological families is the intense shame and guilt that parents who prenatally exposed their child(ren) often carry. This burden can feel overwhelming and incredibly difficult to work through. To these parents, I want to say something that cannot be repeated enough: *No parent ever exposed their child intentionally.*

As a society, we must stop pointing fingers and placing blame on these parents. And parents, you must stop pointing fingers at yourselves. Let yourselves off the hook. The fact that you are reading this book shows how deeply you love your child and how committed you are to becoming an even better parent. The journey isn't about blame; it's about growth, learning, and connection.

You are here, you are trying, and you ROCK.

The most stigmatized disability out there

FASD is one of the most stigmatized disabilities in the world. Society often rushes to blame and shame the parents, particularly the parents who consumed alcohol during pregnancy. While we know prenatal alcohol exposure is the cause of FASD, assigning blame or shame is not helpful—in fact, it's incredibly harmful. This stigma creates barriers to getting the right supports and services for individuals living with FASD and their families.

For many years, a common message from FASD trainers and advocates was that FASD is *100% preventable*. While well intentioned, this message inadvertently fuels shame and guilt in parents who used alcohol while pregnant. It suggests a level of deliberate harm, which is not the case. Most parents who drink during pregnancy either don't realize they are pregnant or are struggling with substance use disorders. This narrative does more harm than good.

As much as we would like to eliminate FASD entirely, the reality is that alcohol is deeply ingrained in societies around the world.

Prohibition in the United States was a colossal failure; alcohol is not going away. There will always be individuals struggling with substance use disorders, and unplanned pregnancies will continue to occur. These are complex social issues, and simplistic solutions like blaming parents or shaming behaviors do not address the root causes.

That said, I am a strong advocate for prevention. We need to increase awareness that *even small amounts of alcohol during all phases of pregnancy can have long-term impacts* on a child. Alcohol exposure during pregnancy has the potential to limit a child's ability to reach their full potential. We must deliver this prevention message clearly and compassionately, without resorting to blame.

Equally important is a focus on *hope and support* for those already affected by FASD. Diagnosis is critical because it opens the door to appropriate interventions, services, and understanding. Families and individuals need to know that help is available and that success is possible with the right supports in place. FASD is a lifelong disability, but with early diagnosis and tailored strategies, we can maximize potential and improve quality of life.

It's time to move past stigma and focus on solutions—prevention, diagnosis, intervention, and building a supportive community for everyone impacted by FASD.

Chapter 3

Amazing Superpowers: Strengths of Those with FASD

Celebrating strengths: Akila's hidden talents

My daughter is an extraordinary individual. She has so many unique gifts, and like many other individuals with fetal alcohol spectrum disorder (FASD), her strengths are all too often overshadowed by her challenges. As a mom, I of course have to start off this section by bragging about my girl. Akila has incredible artistic talent. Her skill in drawing, which only emerged in her early twenties, was revealed when she finally received the right supports and her anxiety decreased. This growth taught me a powerful lesson—the right environment can unlock hidden talents and potential.

Akila also possesses an uncanny sense of direction. We never need to use GPS when she's with us if we are going somewhere she has been before. She has an almost photographic memory of the streets of the Twin Cities (Minneapolis–St Paul), and can give directions better than any navigation app. Alongside these practical strengths, she has a wicked sense of humor and loves to have fun and be silly.

Her long-term memory is unparalleled. She remembers when

all of our birthdays are, and is usually the first person to call on the day. She has very specific and detailed memories of things that happened years ago, which most of us do not remember. Akila is deeply observant, often finding lost items around the house that no one else can locate. She can tell you the make and model of every car which passes us, and she is always right.

Akila is very kind and caring. As a young adult, she lives in a different state from us, but we see her often and talk on the phone or video chat most days. She asks for updates on each of her siblings on our frequent phone calls, and often asks about grandma, aunts, uncles, cousins, co-workers, and others.

Her manners are a huge strength, earning her compliments from teachers, caregivers, and strangers alike. And she's a hard worker, eager to help with projects and contribute meaningfully. These qualities—creativity, kindness, and memory—are just a few examples of the many strengths Akila possesses.

The power of a strengths-based approach

Many individuals with FASD share common gifts, such as a natural ability to connect with younger children. The biggest reason for this is that they are often closer in developmental age to a younger person. For example, there is a 12-year-old-girl I know who prefers playing with 6- to 8-year-olds at recess. This is because she has a hard time fitting in socially with her same-age peers as their brains are functioning at a 12-year-old level while hers is not—even though her expressive language skills match her age of 12.

When I have the opportunity to train school faculty, I encourage the teachers to use service learning as an educational strategy. Service learning is a hands-on educational tool in which students plan and conduct community service projects which are tied to various subjects in the curriculum. Adolescents with FASD learn much better by doing than by listening. Having the 12-year-old girl I mentioned above mentoring and tutoring first-graders is an excellent option to help her gain new skills, share knowledge, and build self-esteem through helping her younger peers.

While therapy can be valuable and may play an important role in a family's journey, it's crucial to understand that therapy alone cannot "fix" a brain injury. The skills and strategies learned in therapy can be incredibly helpful, but it often takes significantly more time for children, adolescents, and even young adults with FASD to internalize and consistently apply these tools. Progress is possible, but it requires patience, consistency, and realistic expectations. As caregivers, shifting our focus from fixing problems to providing compassionate support and understanding is one of the most impactful changes we can make.

It is crucial to find the right therapist. It is pretty rare to find an FASD competent therapist, so I recommend finding one who is trauma competent. Many families I work with have tried numerous modalities, including neurofeedback, eye movement desensitization and reprocessing (EMDR), dialectical behavior therapy (DBT), and others. While some strategies help, the progress is often slow, and not all methods are effective for every individual.

Akila has seen several therapists over the years. By the age of 25, she had worked with at least ten different mental health professionals, none of whom significantly impacted her life in a positive way. In fact, some approaches caused additional stress and disrupted our relationship with her. She eventually refused therapy altogether—a decision we respected, as forcing her to attend sessions often backfired.

This experience taught me that progress takes time and that it's vital to tailor strategies to the individual's needs. It also reinforced the importance of focusing on connection and trust, which form the foundation for any meaningful support.

When creating support plans for individuals with FASD, it's

crucial to adopt a strengths-based approach. Too often, caregivers, educators, and professionals focus on deficits and weaknesses. While addressing challenges is essential, starting with strengths provides a more empowering foundation.

For example, I once worked with a family overwhelmed by therapy appointments for their child. They attended four sessions a week, seeking solutions for every behavioral challenge. When I asked when they had time to simply connect as a family, they admitted they didn't. We decided to shift their focus to spending quality time together, celebrating small victories, and reducing the emphasis on "fixing" problems. The result was a stronger bond between the parents and child—and even some improvements in behavior.

When I'm coaching and working with caregivers, one of the key messages I emphasize is that the responsibility for change often lies with them. As caregivers, our role is to help our children become the best versions of themselves. We provide essentials like clothing, shelter, food, education, love, and structure—everything they need to grow and thrive. It's only natural for us to want to "fix" the challenges they face, not only to make their lives easier but also to reduce the strain on our own!

Shifting focus: From fixing problems to building connections

It can be so easy for caregivers especially to fall into the trap of focusing on the negatives. Even when I was typing up my daughter's strengths, I had to wash from my mind some snarky things I could have added to the strengths. This is due to the fact that the difficult behaviors are so illogical for most adults, and they are hard for us to wrap our heads around. My friend Jeff Noble always says, "You can't convince someone their thinking is off, because their thinking is off." We have a hard time making sense of why a child or adolescent continually cheats when playing a board game; why they may lie when it isn't even beneficial for them; why they use an entire bottle of shampoo in one shower. Trying to use logic to understand unexplainable behaviors will get you every time!

This is why it is so crucial for all supporters in the child's or adolescent's life to understand FASD at a fairly high level. We do better when we know better. Because most individuals with FASD appear typical, talk typically, and often act typically when around others or in public, when they act out inappropriately, we may jump to the conclusion that they are being willfully disobedient.

The assumption is that they are manipulating, controlling, avoiding—all kinds of negative assumptions. I get it. I thought the same thing forever. Those ideas still pop into my head sometimes. But I have learned the hard way that it is rarely intentional. Of course, once in a while they may try to control, manipulate, or avoid something, as they are kids and it is natural for kids to have some behaviors. But the vast majority of the challenges you will encounter with individuals with FASD are not intentional behaviors.

Our school systems unfortunately are more likely to look at the negative aspects of our children, instead of the positives. Not all schools or educators struggle with this mindset, but too many seem to. I need to first of all say that I love educators. I have some good friends who are teachers, and I originally set out to be a teacher. Thankfully when I was in college, I had the revelation that my ADHD self would not do well confined in the walls of a classroom all day, and I pivoted to youth development. Teachers are underpaid, overworked, and overwhelmed with standardized tests and ridiculous amounts of paperwork, especially within the special education programs.

This is not an indictment on schools. This is a reality check. Rarely are educators trained (or anyone for that matter!) on FASD, trauma, or how to better support students with neurodivergence. I have provided FASD training at many schools. I will never forget one training I did in which the caregiver of a student attended as well. At the end of the three-hour training, two educators gave the mother a hug while they were crying and apologizing for things they had said and done, not understanding this mother's child. We do better when we know better.

If I have to see another functional behavior analysis (FBA) or behavior intervention plan (BIP) that states that the child is exhibiting a behavior to seek attention, I may lose it! I had one family whose daughter, aged eight or nine, would act like a horse in class. The FBA and BIP had all kinds of incorrect assumptions about this behavior, including that she was doing it to seek attention. This was just not the case. She would act like a horse when her anxiety rose due to inappropriate expectations from the teachers, the language they used to try to shame her into performing the way they wanted, and other factors within the classroom such as sensory overload.

This was her coping mechanism. Instead, her notes should have read, "Julia uses the coping skill of acting like a horse when she is anxious or stressed. This is a preferred option over screaming, kicking, or cursing. When Julia acts like a horse, this should be an indicator to all staff that Julia is on sensory overload and that the following interventions need to be used: talk little; use a visual cue to attempt to have her use a replacement behavior; and praise her for controlling her brain and body."

Reframing like a rockstar

Raising and supporting individuals with FASD can be incredibly challenging, but it's essential to celebrate small victories. When a child runs away and then they come back home, we celebrate that they came back home and see that as a positive. When an adolescent is asked to wash the dishes and he washes the dishes and leaves the silverware and cups dirty, we celebrate that he washed the dishes (and we realize we need to use a different language for a concrete-brained person!). When a child calls you 50 times a day, we celebrate that she feels connected to you (but please don't answer all 50 calls).

I know a family who had a young adult with FASD. He struggled with taking things that were not his, which we refer to as "stealing" in society. This young adult got a job repossessing cars and he told his parents that it kind of helped satisfy the need he had to take things. I thought that was fascinating and insightful of this young man. For many of our youth who do steal, it is more of an impulse control challenge, which we will cover in Chapter 9.

When most people observe a child's behavior, they often assume it is willful or intentional. However, in the context of FASD, what appears to be a behavior is actually a symptom of brain injury. By learning to reframe these actions as symptoms rather than intentional behaviors, we can approach the child with greater patience and respond more effectively. Reframing is a skill that took me time to develop, but it's one I've since mastered.

When my daughter is using a way louder voice than she should in a situation, I may say something like, "I love your enthusiasm" or, "This sounds like something you are passionate about, by the volume of your voice." Often she is not even aware of how loud she is. When she has all of her belongings strewn all over the living room, I might say, "Wow, looks like you have been having fun!" or, "Goodness, you have had such a busy and productive day, you had to leave your things all over. Let's pick them up together." When Akila is refusing to attend an appointment or meeting, I may say something like, "I am so proud of how good you have got at advocating for yourself for things you want to do and don't want to do." After that, I may see if I can gently encourage her to attend the appointment or meeting, but I have learned not to push it too much or it will backfire and she will end up escalating.

Common strengths of individuals with FASD

1. **Strong expressive language skills:** Many individuals with FASD excel in expressive language. This is one of their most noticeable strengths and often leads to misunderstandings, as they can appear more mature or capable than they actually are.

2. **Forgiving nature:** Due to working memory deficits, individuals with FASD often let go of negative experiences quickly, making them less likely to hold grudges and more inclined to forgive easily.

3. **Energetic:** Most children with FASD are full of energy and rarely have an "off" button. This high energy level can be a strength, although it may shift during adolescence or young adulthood for some individuals.

4. **Friendly and likable:** These individuals often have fun and engaging personalities, making them naturally friendly and likable. However, when emotional regulation challenges arise—such as outbursts or rages—this strength can sometimes be overshadowed.

5. **Observant:** Many children with FASD often have an incredible ability to notice details, such as spotting missing items or changes in their environment. Their "eagle eyes" can be a valuable strength.

6. **Talented in arts, music, or athletics:** Many individuals with FASD have notable talents in artistic, musical, or athletic pursuits. These abilities often flourish when they are nurtured and supported.

7. **Resilient:** Despite facing significant daily challenges, individuals with FASD show remarkable resilience. They endure hardships that would overwhelm most people, yet their struggles are often unseen or unrecognized by anyone outside their caregiving circle.

8. **Good with technology:** Individuals with FASD often have a natural affinity for technology. They are adept at navigating devices and solving tech problems—sometimes bypassing firewalls with ease. While this can be a challenge, it also makes them a valuable resource for teaching their caregivers tech skills.

Unlocking potential

Akila's journey has taught me that the right supports, coupled with a focus on strengths, can unlock potential we never imagined. Her story is a testament to the resilience and brilliance of individuals with FASD—and a reminder that, with the right perspective, we can all make a difference in their lives.

As caregivers and professionals, we must remember that these struggles are not intentional. Children and adolescents with FASD are not waking up each day planning to frustrate their parents, teachers, and peers. Their behaviors are almost always symptoms of an invisible brain injury—a reality that requires patience, understanding, and compassion.

Chapter 4

The FASD Puzzle: Piecing Together Symptoms

Common symptoms

It's a common misconception that the behavioral and learning challenges exhibited by individuals with fetal alcohol spectrum disorder (FASD) stem from willful disobedience or poor decision-making that they have full control over. While there are times when behaviors may be intentional, the vast majority of challenges are actually symptoms of their brain injury. When we begin to view these behaviors as symptoms rather than deliberate actions, it becomes easier to respond with patience, offer grace, and manage our own frustration. This perspective shift allows us to approach adolescents with greater understanding and compassion, reducing anger and fostering a more supportive environment.

Not every individual with FASD has every symptom, but there are some which are very common and we will cover them below.

Inconsistency and working memory

Many children and adolescents with FASD exhibit extreme inconsistencies in their knowledge, abilities, and attitudes. This inconsistency is primarily due to the impact of prenatal alcohol exposure on the corpus callosum—a bundle of nerve fibers that facilitates communication between the left and right hemispheres of the brain. Research on FASD has shown that, through specific MRI imaging techniques, damage to the corpus callosum is sometimes visible in specific slices of MRIs which are only used for research.[1] While such imaging is not used for diagnostic purposes due to various limitations, it serves as an important tool for advancing our understanding of FASD in research settings.

When Akila was in elementary school, we worked hard to help her memorize the multiplication tables, but it was a real struggle. Because of her limited attention span, we kept our practice sessions to just ten minutes at a time. I remember focusing on the two-times table with her. At the end of a session, she would seem to have it down perfectly. Yet, just 30 minutes later, if I asked her what it was, she would look at me blankly, unable to recall the answer. An hour later, I'd ask again, and this time she'd reply, "Four. Why do you always ask me?" It was not until years later that I finally understood this was due to her corpus callosum damage, and was not her being lazy or avoidant.

During this time, we hadn't yet understood the importance of using connected and relational strategies. Instead, we often fell back on unhelpful, shaming language without realizing the harm it could cause. I would say things like, "Try harder," "Think!" or even, "Are you kidding me?" I'm deeply ashamed to admit that I might have even asked, "Are you trying to act dumb?" Looking back, I wince at the thought of those words, recognizing now how much they ignored the underlying challenges Akila was facing and how damaging they could have been to her confidence.

Once we began to truly understand her brain and how the effects of her brain injury manifested, we decided to let go of the goal of memorizing the multiplication tables. It wasn't about giving up on her ability to learn but about protecting her self-esteem and preserving her joy of learning. Could she have eventually memorized more of the tables? Possibly. But at what cost? If we had continued to push her beyond her capacity, she likely would have grown increasingly frustrated, not just with math, but with school and learning as a whole. By choosing to prioritize her emotional well-being over rigid academic goals, we were able to create an environment where she could feel supported and capable.

This inconsistency goes beyond just memory—it also affects a child's ability to complete tasks and demonstrate their knowledge on specific topics. A child with FASD might successfully complete a task with minimal assistance one day but struggle to do the same task the next day. This variability is often tied to how their brain processes information, particularly when the corpus callosum isn't firing correctly. These challenges are more pronounced when the individual is dealing with anxiety, whether it's a small amount or an overwhelming wave. Anxiety seems to disrupt their brain's ability to communicate effectively, amplifying the inconsistencies in their abilities. Recognizing this helps us approach these moments with greater patience and understanding.

Anxiety

We've all experienced anxiety at some point in our lives, even if we don't have a diagnosable generalized anxiety disorder. Common situations that provoke anxiety include giving a speech in front of a group, interviewing for a new job, driving in a snowstorm, or seeing flashing lights in the rearview mirror, thinking we might be pulled over. For those without an anxiety disorder, these feelings are typically short-lived, occurring only during the stressful moment.

When we experience anxiety, it triggers a cascade of physiological and neurological responses that affect both our brain and body. The heart rate increases, pumping blood more rapidly to prepare the body for action, and this increase in circulation raises body temperature, which is why people often perspire during stressful moments. Alongside this, blood sugar levels and blood pressure rise as part of the body's "fight or flight" response, ensuring that energy is readily available for immediate use. Muscles also tense up, preparing the body to either confront the stressor or escape from it. These physical responses are closely tied to heightened brain activity, which shifts into overdrive during times of anxiety.

In these moments, the brain prioritizes survival instincts over higher-level cognitive functions. The prefrontal cortex, which governs decision-making, problem-solving, and memory, becomes less active as the amygdala, the brain's emotional response center, takes the lead. This shift makes it challenging to think clearly, recall important information, or make sound decisions. Instead, the brain focuses on immediate threats, which can result in a narrowed perception of the situation and an overwhelming sense of urgency or fear.

After the stressful event passes—such as arriving home safely after navigating a dangerous snowstorm—the body begins the process of returning to its baseline state, a phase known as regulation or recovery. This transition isn't instantaneous. The elevated heart rate slows, blood sugar and blood pressure levels stabilize, and tense muscles relax. Similarly, the brain recalibrates, restoring balance to its functions and allowing the prefrontal cortex to resume its normal activity. However, this recovery process takes time and varies from person to person based on factors like individual stress resilience, overall health, and the intensity of the anxiety-inducing event.

Understanding this process is crucial for managing stress effectively, both for ourselves and for the children in our care. Recognizing the signs of heightened anxiety—the racing heart, quickened breathing, tense muscles, and difficulty concentrating—provides a valuable opportunity to intervene before the stress escalates further. Knowing that the body and brain need time to recover can empower caregivers, professionals, and individuals to approach the situation with patience and intention.

Engaging in calming practices, such as deep breathing, mindfulness, or gentle physical activity, can be highly effective in facilitating a return to a calm state. These techniques help to reset the nervous system, bringing the body out of "fight or flight" mode and back into balance. For children, especially those with trauma histories or neurodevelopmental conditions such as FASD, the role of caregivers and professionals is even more vital. Children often lack the ability to recognize and articulate their anxiety, making it essential for the adults in their lives to be attuned to their needs and emotional states.

When a child is experiencing anxiety, meeting them with connection and calmness is key. Rather than reacting with frustration or escalating the situation, we must approach them in a non-stressful, understanding way. This connected approach might include getting down to the child's eye level, using a soft tone of voice, offering comforting physical gestures like a gentle touch (if welcomed), or simply validating their feelings with empathetic statements such as, "I can see this is really hard for you right now."

By providing this kind of co-regulation, caregivers and professionals can help the child begin to regulate their own emotions. Co-regulation is a process where the calmness and stability of the caregiver act as a model for the child's own nervous system, guiding them toward a state of greater balance. This is particularly important for children who struggle with self-regulation due to developmental or neurological challenges.

In these moments, it's also helpful to offer simple, actionable steps the child can take to regain a sense of control and calm. This might include leading them in a breathing exercise ("Let's take three big breaths together"), suggesting a sensory activity like squeezing a stress ball, or even helping them move to a quieter, more soothing environment. My colleague and FASD expert, Dr. Michael Harris, has taught me and many caregivers about PQ reps, another mindfulness strategy. Search PQ reps online and give them a try.

Anxiety experts emphasize that we often miss the mark when we focus solely on stopping an undesirable behavior in the moment. Instead, we should dig deeper to understand what is driving the anxiety behind the behavior. Our energy should be directed toward addressing the root cause of the anxiety rather than the surface-level actions.

For example, if a child is calling you names and swearing, rather than concentrating on what they're saying, consider what might be causing their stress at that moment. Are they anxious because a babysitter is coming soon and they struggle with transitions? Or did the noisy, overstimulating bus ride home from school put them into sensory overload? By identifying and addressing the source of their anxiety, we can make more meaningful progress than simply telling them to stop the behavior—which is unlikely to have much impact.

In Chapter 6, I'll introduce the BEARS acronym, a practical tool to help dig deeper into identifying and addressing the underlying symptoms of anxiety.

Wrong words

When their anxiety is high, children with FASD often struggle to find the right words to express what they are feeling. Years ago, I worked with a school in the suburbs of the Twin Cities (Minneapolis–St Paul) in Minnesota where a first-grade girl would come to school every morning complaining that she was starving and thirsty. The school believed her parents were withholding proper nutrition to avoid bedwetting and was preparing to report them to child protective services for neglect.

After interviewing the parents, I didn't think the parents were neglecting this young girl, so I spent a day shadowing her, even riding the bus with her. I observed the stress she experienced during the loud and chaotic bus ride. The hallways were similarly overwhelming, and even as she entered her classroom, her anxiety was visible as she placed her coat and backpack in her cubby. I watched her approach the teacher, saying she was hungry and thirsty. The teacher, familiar with this routine, wrote her a pass to the nurse's office.

In the quiet, calm environment of the nurse's office, I saw the girl visibly relax. The nurse gave her a granola bar and water while chatting pleasantly, and within minutes, the girl returned to class regulated and ready to learn. She wasn't starving or overly thirsty; she had simply found a way to access an accommodation that helped her regulate after sensory overload from the bus, hallways, and unstructured morning routine. She didn't have the words to explain what she was truly experiencing.

I recommended that she be given special education transportation to reduce the stress of the bus ride and that she start her mornings with a structured visit to the nurse's office for a snack and drink. Her parents were more than willing to provide granola bars to support this solution.

This experience made me reflect on word choices and how children use language. When a child tells an adult they are hungry, thirsty, hot, or cold, the adult naturally tries to address these concrete issues. However, I began to realize that many times, when my daughter Akila used these words, they didn't align with the actual situation. For example, she might say she was starving just five minutes after finishing a large meal. My instinct was to argue and tell her there was no way she could be hungry, which often escalated into a full-blown meltdown.

It eventually clicked that when Akila used these words in a moment that didn't make sense, it was often her way of signaling anxiety she couldn't articulate. I started a new approach, saying, "Are you hot/cold/hungry/full? You're feeling something—let's pause and figure out what it is." Most of the time, she wasn't experiencing what she said but rather underlying anxiety. This small shift in how I responded helped us uncover the true source of her feelings without unnecessary conflict.

Over time, Akila began to adopt this practice herself. Sometimes now, she'll pause and say, "Wait, am I hot/cold/hungry/full? What am I feeling?" Reflecting on this, I can only imagine how many rages and misunderstandings we could have avoided had we used this approach her entire life. The impact on her self-esteem and our relationship could have been profound, underscoring the importance of looking beyond the words to understand what children with FASD are truly trying to communicate.

Struggling with abstract concepts

Think about a toddler's brain—they are incredibly concrete thinkers. Toddlers and young children struggle to understand abstract concepts, and this trait can persist far beyond childhood for individuals with FASD, often lasting their entire lives. This concrete way of thinking is humorously illustrated in memes and jokes about how literal thinkers perceive the world. Many in the FASD community liken individuals with FASD to Amelia Bedelia, the popular children's book character who takes everything literally—she might just be the poster child for concrete thinking!

This difficulty in grasping abstract concepts can lead to significant frustration, miscommunications, and even poor performance on tests or assignments. For someone who thinks concretely, everything is interpreted literally, with little room for nuance or gray areas. This black-and-white perspective makes navigating society a challenge. People may sometimes laugh at teens or adults with FASD, believing they are intentionally being funny, when in reality, they are simply struggling to understand or process an abstract concept. This misunderstanding can add to their frustration and create unnecessary barriers in their social interactions.

Mathematics

Mathematics is one of the most common subjects our kids struggle with—and it has been a significant challenge for me throughout my life. I managed early elementary math well enough, but word problems? No, thank you. Even now, they make my anxiety spike. And algebra? Who thought it was a good idea to mix numbers and letters? Numbers belong in math; letters belong in reading and writing. For someone who is a concrete thinker and struggles with abstract concepts, combining the two makes no sense at all.

Research using imaging equipment has shown that prenatal alcohol exposure impacts the areas of the brain essential for mathematical processing.[2] This explains why math can be such a challenge for many individuals with FASD. Of course, there are exceptions. I knew a young man with FASD who, at 18, completed an online precalculus course through a community college and earned a B without any outside assistance. Frankly, I couldn't do that even today!

For the majority of our kids, however, math becomes increasingly difficult as they reach secondary school. While some may be able to handle it, many cannot, and it's critical that educators pivot their focus to teaching practical, life-skills math. This approach can better support these students, equipping them with essential tools for everyday life rather than forcing abstract concepts that are unlikely to be useful or comprehensible.

Without appropriate accommodations and modifications in math and science, many of these kids will end up hating school and struggling with feelings of inadequacy and low self-worth. They may internalize their difficulties, believing they are "stupid" simply because they cannot grasp abstract concepts or keep up with their peers. This can have a lasting impact on their confidence and willingness to engage in learning, highlighting the importance of tailoring education to meet their unique needs.

Sensory processing

Most individuals with FASD also face sensory processing challenges—something I've come to recognize about myself over the past several years. I struggle with tags on clothing, regulating my body temperature, sensitivity to light (which leads to frequent headaches), an aversion to slippery food textures, and an acute sensitivity to smells and odors. These struggles are common among people who were prenatally exposed to alcohol.

Sensory processing disorder occurs when the brain has difficulty interpreting sensory information such as sights, smells, sounds, tastes, and textures. This misprocessing often leads to sensory overload, which can manifest as behavioral issues and emotional dysregulation. For instance, something seemingly minor might provoke an intense emotional response in a child or teen because their brain is overwhelmed by sensory input. Understanding these sensory challenges is essential to supporting individuals with FASD and helping them navigate their world more comfortably.

I have several memories of times when odors sent Akila into sensory overload. When we were driving down the highway and passing a road construction site where they were laying a new pavement, that thick smell of tar would totally dysregulate her. I remember vacuuming once and getting something stuck in the vacuum. That burnt rubber smell permeated through the house and she totally lost it. I actually packed all the kids in the car and left the house as she was so dysregulated.

Time blindness

Many children and adolescents with FASD experience something called "time blindness." While many of them can read an analog clock, recite the time they're supposed to be somewhere, or agree to get off a device in 30 minutes, this doesn't mean they truly understand what 30 minutes feels like. For most neurotypical teenagers and adults, this ability to sense the passage of time is an abstract skill that comes naturally. We instinctively know what five minutes, an hour, or an eight-hour workday feels like. For individuals with time blindness, this lack of awareness can lead to significant challenges.

For example, difficulties with time perception may contribute to incontinence issues. Most people, when they feel the first signs of needing to urinate, can gauge how long they have before it becomes urgent. However, children and adolescents with time blindness often cannot make this connection, leading to accidents.

Time blindness also complicates agreements around time limits. If a child agrees to stop using a device after 30 minutes, they might not feel as though they've had enough time when the timer goes off—even if the time was accurate. This can lead to frustration and outbursts, leaving caregivers bewildered because the child agreed to the limit.

They often do not have strong time management skills. If the caregiver and child have agreed on one hour on a device, and the child refuses to get off after one hour, it may be because they just started a video game or a video when there were ten minutes left and it is a 28-minute video. Due to their rigid thinking and lack of flexibility, getting off before the game or video ends is very difficult for them.

The key to managing time blindness is to make time visible. Tools like sand timers, visual countdown apps, or clocks with disappearing red sections (representing time passing) can help individuals see and better grasp the concept of elapsed time. These strategies help bridge the gap between an abstract concept and a tangible experience, making it easier for them to feel and respond to the passing of time.

Time blindness can also lead to anticipatory stress. When children with FASD have an upcoming event they are focused on—whether they are feeling fear, excitement, or a mix of both—it can cause significant stress and anxiety. For example, I know a family whose 18-year-old daughter became fixated on her graduation party starting in September of her senior year. It was all she could talk about for months. Similarly, many children with FASD become obsessed with their birthdays or holidays, and this intense focus often results in heightened anxiety.

Using visual and concrete methods to help them count down to the big event can be incredibly effective in managing this anticipatory stress. Tools like countdown calendars, visual timers, or even tangible representations of time (such as removing a paper link from a chain each day) can help them better process and manage the lead-up to these highly anticipated moments.

Money management

Money, as an abstract concept, can be exceptionally challenging for individuals with FASD to grasp. Understanding the value of money, such as the difference between a five-dollar bill, a twenty-dollar bill, or a hundred-dollar bill, is difficult for many in this population. In today's increasingly digital world, money is even more abstract. With a few taps on a phone, an item can arrive at the front door within hours—kids often don't even witness money being exchanged anymore.

One of the most significant triggers for children and adolescents with FASD is not getting what they want immediately. This is similar to the tantrums seen in toddlers, who struggle with delayed gratification. When Akila was younger, fake fingernails were a constant trigger. I used to blog about our challenges, and I remember someone suggesting we buy her press-on nails from the drugstore. Of course, we had tried that, along with taking her to the nail salon. Yet within 24 to 48 hours—or sometimes less—she would pull the nails off due to sensory issues, and the cycle of perseverating (obsessing) over fake fingernails would start all over again.

I could have stocked an endless supply of fake nails, and it still wouldn't have been enough. This difficulty in understanding limits is common among individuals with FASD and often extends into adulthood. For instance, I know of a family whose teenage son found a submarine online for $75,000 and could not grasp why his parents wouldn't buy it for him (not to mention where they would store it, we are talking about an actual full-sized submarine, not a model!). This lack of comprehension around financial limits and realistic expectations highlights the ongoing challenges faced by those with FASD and their families.

An incident from Akila's elementary school years highlights how abstract the concept of money can be. I was helping a friend with deposits for their dance studio, and one evening, I left a pile of checks and cash on my desk to finish in the morning. When I returned, the cash was gone, and I knew where it was. At school, I found Akila in the cafeteria handing out twenty-dollar bills to older girls. When I approached, she defensively said, "What? I didn't do anything!" before I'd even spoken. As we talked, girls started lining up to return the money, and I was able to recover the $300. Akila, who was in fourth grade at the time, had no idea how much money she had given away, or its value.

This incident, and many like it, underscore the difficulties individuals with FASD face in understanding the abstract nature of money, its value, and its limits—challenges that require ongoing patience and creative strategies to address.

Impulse control

As I type, the words *impulse control* make me shudder, as the lack of it has caused major challenges in our family. Most individuals with FASD struggle with impulse control to varying degrees—some mild, others severe. Impulse control is one of the core executive functioning skills, and when it's impaired, it can lead to issues such as stealing, sexual impulsivity, verbal aggression, and even physical aggression. In Chapter 1, I shared how we threw away Akila's blanket in an attempt to teach her not to steal. Akila has always had significant struggles with impulse control, but now she is in her early twenties, we are beginning to see progress. This gives me hope that with time and support, our kids can improve.

The lack of impulse control continues to create challenges for many individuals with FASD. For instance, they might say things that should have stayed inside their heads, leading to name-calling, swearing, or behavior that comes across as disrespectful. However, when we step back and realize that their brain is essentially "on fire" in those moments, it becomes easier to reframe the behavior as a symptom of their condition and to respond with more patience. When Akila gets into her name-calling phase, it no longer fazes me because I've learned that most of what she says in those moments doesn't reflect her true feelings. Even if her words seem deeply personal, I know they usually aren't. I embrace the Q-TIP philosophy, which stands for "Quit Taking It Personally."

Sexual impulsivity is another significant challenge for many individuals with FASD, and it's a particularly sensitive and complex issue to address. Many caregivers and professionals shy away from discussing it, but it's essential that we do. Imagine a 12-year-old boy with the typical prepubescent hormones of his age but the developmental maturity of a six-year-old. This mismatch is a recipe for disaster, and without proper guidance and support, it can lead to significant difficulties for the child and those around them. Addressing this topic openly and with understanding is critical to helping our children navigate these challenges safely and appropriately.

Comprehension

I had never really thought about comprehension in my early life, but now I think about it pretty often. So many with FASD, even those with IQs in the average or high average range, do not always comprehend things which we think they would. They get really good at "masking," making it look as if they comprehend and understand something they maybe don't. All of us have done this. Maybe you are at a dinner party and someone has explained something to you and you did not understand. You asked for clarification and they clarify. You still don't understand, but you pretend you do, so that you can move on and not feel dumb. This is in essence what our kids do, but I think we would be surprised at how often they do this.

Richard Lavoie created a great training to help people better understand learning disabilities. In his video titled *How Difficult Can This Be? The F.A.T. City Workshop*, Lavoie uses several activities which help participants feel what it is like to have a disability.[3] One activity is a powerful tool to help us understand comprehension and masking. Read the story below and then answer the first four questions— don't cheat and look at the answers!

> Last serny, Fingledobe and Pribin were in the nerd-link treppering gloopy caples and cleaming burly greps.
>
> Suddenly a ditty strezzle boofed into Fingledobe's tresk. Pribin glaped and glaped.
>
> "Oh Fingledobe!" He Chifed, "That ditty strezzle is tunning in your grep!"

Here are the questions you now need to answer:

1. What were the names of the characters?
2. What happened to Fingledobe's tresk?
3. What did Pribin then do?
4. When did the story take place?

Have you answered them all? Here are the answers:

1. Fingledobe and Pribin.
2. A ditty strezzle boofed into it.
3. He glaped and glaped.
4. Last serny.

The final question is, what does this story mean? We don't really know but the point of this exercise is to highlight how we can read a story and answer the questions correctly, yet still not fully comprehend its meaning. We may be savvy or skilled enough to provide the right answers, but that doesn't mean we truly understand. This is a common experience for individuals with FASD, often occurring multiple times a day.

This disconnect frequently leads to significant miscommunication. As caregivers or professionals, we assume they understand what we are asking or expecting, but in reality, they may be masking their confusion. When they fail to meet expectations, we become frustrated and may punish them for not following through, unaware that the issue stems from a lack of comprehension rather than defiance. Recognizing this pattern is crucial to fostering better communication and reducing unnecessary conflict.

I was a legal guardian for a young adult for a few years, and during that time, I brought him to an intake meeting for adult mental-health case management. The meeting lasted a little over an hour, and he did a great job staying engaged. We developed a solid case plan, and I thought the meeting had gone well.

On the drive back to his group home, I asked him what he thought about the meeting. His response surprised me: he said he had no idea what we had been talking about. I asked a few clarifying questions and realized he was genuinely clueless about most of the discussion.

What he said next was a light bulb moment for me. He explained, "I just said whatever I thought you both wanted to hear so that the meeting would be over." I was dumbfounded. It made me rethink how I approached similar situations.

I realized Akila had been doing the same thing for years, especially in settings like Individualized Education Program (IEP) meetings, case management discussions, and therapy sessions. It wasn't just limited to formal meetings, though; this pattern extended into daily life and routine tasks.

For example, an adolescent might say they brought home their homework to study for a midterm. In reality, they may have brought home assignments for other subjects but not the one with the test. They aren't intentionally lying—it's more about masking or not completely understanding the question.

This masking behavior is particularly noticeable in therapy. Many of our kids have been in therapy for so long that they've mastered "therapy speak." They know the right things to say and can often run verbal circles around even experienced therapists. When they don't have the "right" answer, this is often when confabulation begins—a topic I'll cover in more detail in Chapter 8.

Generalizing

Think about how often we rely on generalization in our daily lives. Generalizing is the ability to transfer knowledge from one situation to another that is similar but not identical. For many individuals with FASD, this skill is significantly impaired, leaving them vulnerable and unable to learn from past mistakes the way a neurotypical person might. This inability to generalize also contributes to struggles in subjects like math and science, where applying learned concepts to new but related problems is a constant requirement.

For example, a simple change in how a math problem is presented—such as moving from a vertical equation to a horizontal one—can confuse someone with FASD. I recall observing a student in a math class while providing FASD support to several school districts. A paraprofessional had walked the student through solving a problem and then asked her to apply the same formula to the next four problems while he helped another student. However, when he returned, the student had not worked on any of the problems. The para was frustrated with the student for not trying.

I approached the student and asked why she hadn't worked on the other problems. She responded, "They're not the same." I then reviewed the original problem the paraprofessional had used to teach the student and rewrote one of the new problems using the exact same numbers. Once it looked identical to the original, she was able to solve it correctly using the formula. The student's thinking was so concrete that she couldn't generalize the process to problems that were even slightly different, unless the numbers matched exactly.

An adolescent boy eagerly wanted the responsibility of retrieving the mail each day after it was delivered. Their family's mailbox was located across a busy street. His parent carefully worked with him, teaching him how to look both ways and cross the street safely. Together, they practiced the steps repeatedly until he felt confident. On his first solo attempt, he successfully looked both ways, crossed the street, and retrieved the mail. However, on his way back, he ran straight across the street without looking, narrowly avoiding danger.

The parent realized that while he had learned how to cross the street safely in one direction, he hadn't been able to apply that skill when returning. This is a *classic example of a lack of generalization*—the inability to transfer learned skills or strategies to new but similar situations.

For individuals with FASD, learning something in one context doesn't guarantee they'll understand how to apply it in another, even when it seems intuitive to others. Recognizing this challenge can help caregivers and educators take a step back, break tasks into smaller steps, and explicitly teach each part of a process—like crossing the street in both directions. It's not about intelligence or effort; it's about how the brain processes and applies information differently. This story is a reminder that patience, repetition, and understanding are key when helping individuals with FASD build skills that truly stick.

Generalization challenges can also lead to risky situations in real life. Years ago, I worked with a family whose 21-year-old son left the house one night to buy cannabis on the streets. A car pulled up, and the young man talked with the driver for several minutes before mentioning he was looking to purchase some weed. The driver claimed to have some at home and invited him into the car. The young man agreed, but once inside, the driver pulled over and robbed him at knifepoint.

Later, the father called to share what happened and said he believed his son had learned his lesson, as he seemed very shaken by the robbery. He asked for my thoughts, and I told him I was confident his son wouldn't get in *that* man's car again. However, if a different person in a different car approached him under similar circumstances, it could happen all over again.

This is a common pattern: many individuals with FASD struggle to recognize patterns or apply generalized advice like "Don't get in the car with a stranger." For a concrete thinker, what defines "a stranger"? Someone they've spoken with for a few minutes might feel like a close friend. I've seen kids excitedly tell their caregivers about a "new best friend," only to be unable to provide basic details like the person's name or where they live.

A few years later, I ran into that same father at a conference and asked if his son had learned from the incident. He replied, "No, he's still putting himself in dangerous situations." This underscores the critical need to tailor guidance and interventions for individuals with FASD. They require specific, clear, and consistent strategies to navigate these situations safely.

Sleep

Sleep is a critical brain function. The pineal gland in our brain plays a key role by signaling the body to produce melatonin, the hormone that regulates sleep cycles. For individuals with FASD, prenatal alcohol exposure disrupts this process, making sleep a significant challenge. Many struggle with falling asleep, staying asleep, or experiencing night terrors, particularly those who have endured early life trauma.

When Akila was young, we tried everything to improve her sleep while avoiding medications. We limited screen time, used essential oils in a diffuser, and included bath time and calm book reading in her bedtime routine. Unfortunately, none of these strategies were enough. The breaking point came when, at seven years old, Akila left our home at 2 a.m. to walk to a gas station and buy gum. This event pushed us to start her on sleep medication the very next day and we also installed door alarms.

Sleep deprivation affects everyone's ability to function, and this is especially true for individuals with FASD. When they are already predisposed to challenging behaviors, lack of sleep exacerbates those issues. Moreover, if the kids aren't sleeping, neither are the caregivers. Exhaustion makes it incredibly difficult to provide the connected, relational care that children with FASD need.

If sleep challenges persist despite trying various strategies, it may be necessary to involve medical professionals. Addressing sleep problems often has a ripple effect, improving not only their rest but also their anxiety levels, mood, and overall behavior, which can make a world of difference for both the child and the family.

Social skills

When we consider the developmentally scattered profile common among children and adolescents with FASD, it's no surprise that their social skills often lag behind those of their same-age peers. This can be particularly confusing because their expressive language skills are typically a strength. As a result, we may mistakenly assume they will have strong social skills, but that's rarely the case.

For instance, if a child is ten years old but functioning closer to the developmental level of a five-year-old, they're likely to struggle socially with same-age peers. Most children with FASD excel at interacting with adults. My daughter, for example, loved visiting the offices at her schools and built strong relationships with the secretaries. Talking with adults was far less stressful for her than trying to connect with same-age peers, with whom she struggled to relate. Adults, especially those who work with children, are often skilled at meeting kids where they are, developmentally, whereas peers typically don't have that ability.

As I mentioned in the chapter on strengths, many children and adolescents with FASD do well with younger children because their developmental profile aligns more closely with that age group. This is directly tied to their social skill deficits and helps explain why they often find interactions with younger kids easier and more enjoyable than those with their same-age peers.

Dementia and FASD: Parallels in behavior and understanding

I have a friend whose mother passed away years ago from Alzheimer's, a devastating form of dementia. In her final years, she lived in a memory care facility, and the family took turns taking her to church. One Sunday, her 21-year-old grandson brought her to mass.

As Catholics, they went up for communion during the service. When the priest offered her the communion wafer, saying, "Body of Christ," her response shocked her grandson: "I don't want that fucking wrinkly wafer!" Embarrassed, he whispered, "Grandma, it's okay." She replied loudly, "Fuck if it is!" The priest, trying to be patient, gave her another wafer, which she also deemed unacceptable, leading to an even louder string of F-bombs. Eventually, she had to be escorted out of the church.

When my friend told me this story, we both laughed hysterically. In caregiving, laughter is sometimes the only way to cope with the challenging and absurd moments. Then she said something that stopped me in my tracks: "This story reminds me of all the ones you tell about Akila." She was right.

This really got me thinking about Alzheimer's and how it manifests behaviorally. As my friend's mom's disease progressed, she would become physically aggressive, lashing out at staff and family when she was frustrated. It's important to note that not everyone with Alzheimer's exhibits physical aggression—just as not all individuals with FASD do. However, similar behaviors often emerge in both conditions, offering striking parallels.

For instance, stealing can be a common behavior in memory care, even among individuals who have never stolen before. Food hoarding is another frequent occurrence, even in those who have never experienced food insecurity. And then there's lying—though in memory care, we often recognize this as *confabulation*, where the brain fills in memory gaps with false information. (I'll cover confabulation in more depth in Chapter 8.)

These behaviors aren't willful or intentional—they're symptoms of the brain's compromised function. Understanding this can help us approach both Alzheimer's and FASD with greater empathy and compassion.

This realization sparked a shift in how I viewed FASD. I began to reflect on Alzheimer's and its behavioral manifestations. The behaviors associated with Alzheimer's—aggression, stealing, hoarding, confabulation—are strikingly similar to those we see in individuals with FASD. Both conditions are rooted in brain function, and the resulting behaviors are rarely intentional.

However, there's a fundamental difference. With Alzheimer's, we knew the person before their brain was affected. We know who they were, how they behaved, and the values they held. My friend's mother would never have dropped F-bombs at a priest before her diagnosis. This memory allowed the family to give her grace, patience, and understanding because they could clearly separate her disease from her identity.

Children with FASD don't have the luxury of a "before." They were born with a brain injury, and their behaviors have always been influenced by it. But doesn't that make them even more deserving of grace, patience, and understanding?

Do you think the memory care staff punished my friend's mother for her outburst at church? Did they take away her phone, revoke her screen time, or bar her from the next community outing? Of course not. They understood that her behavior was beyond her control and not intentional.

Changing how we respond

This comparison made me rethink how we approach behaviors in individuals with FASD. If we can show compassion and avoid punitive measures with dementia patients, we can do the same for our children. Instead of consequences, we need connection. Instead of judgment, we need understanding.

Caregiving isn't easy—whether it's for a loved one with dementia or a child with FASD. But shifting our mindset to focus on the brain injury, rather than viewing behaviors as willful or manipulative, changes everything. It allows us to respond with empathy and to prioritize relationships over punishment—because every person, no matter their age or diagnosis, deserves to be treated with dignity and grace.

Chapter 5

Building Bridges: Moving Away from Traditional Consequence-Based Approaches

Parenting how we were parented

Most caregivers parent the way they were parented—whether they feel good about their childhood or not. We often try to do things differently in areas where we found our parents' approach frustrating, but we tend to stick to the same basic philosophies. I can clearly remember my teenage self vowing, *I will not be like my parents.* Yet here I am—just like my parents in so many ways.

The majority of caregivers worldwide parent by relying on consequences, punishments, and logic. However, logic and fetal alcohol spectrum disorder (FASD) do not go hand in hand, to say the least. I always feel a deep sense of empathy for caregivers who have successfully raised neurotypical children and then try to use those same strategies with children and adolescents who have FASD or whose brains have been impacted by trauma. What worked before simply doesn't work now.

It's often said that the definition of insanity is doing the same thing repeatedly and expecting a different outcome. This is the vicious cycle I see so many families—and even professionals—fall into. Most of us start off using consequence-based strategies, and far too often, we cling to them long after they've proven ineffective, sometimes causing harm in the process.

As I reflect on our own journey, I'm still baffled at why it took us so long to pivot. Why didn't we stop using consequences sooner? We thought they would teach our daughter to stop certain behaviors or motivate her to start doing things like cleaning her room. Instead, we ended up caught in an endless loop of frustration and disconnection, when what she really needed was something entirely different.

There are a few reasons why caregivers of kids with FASD get stuck using traditional consequence-based strategies. First, it's familiar. Most of us were raised with consequences and punishments, and it's still the default parenting approach for the majority of caregivers. These strategies often work quite well for neurotypical individuals. Many adults look back at their own upbringing and think, *I turned out fine, so this must be the right way to parent.* This mindset is especially common among adoptive and foster caregivers who have successfully raised neurotypical children. It worked for them before, so they naturally assume it will work again.

Second, I believe we're born with an innate instinct to think punishment is an effective way to teach someone to stop doing something. At a surface level, it feels logical. Our society reinforces this belief through its structures—education, the justice system, the workplace—all of which rely on consequences as a means of behavior modification.

When I think back to the years we used consequences with Akila, or when I observe other families doing the same, I'm fascinated by how long we kept trying it, despite how rarely it worked. When we sought professional help from therapists and doctors, their advice was often to double down: "Be more consistent," they'd say, "Structure the punishments more clearly." And we followed that advice.

One of my favorite quotes is from author and educator Walter Barbe: "If you've told a child a thousand times and they still haven't learned, it is not the child who is the slow learner." I reference this quote often—probably up to five times a week—when training families and professionals on FASD. It encapsulates one of the biggest challenges for caregivers: getting stuck on the hamster wheel of consequences. They try the same approach over and over, hoping for a different outcome, but the results rarely improve.

One of the reasons families have such a hard time stepping off this hamster wheel is that they don't know what else to do. It's easy to point out what isn't working, but without viable alternatives, caregivers feel lost and overwhelmed.

In this chapter, we explain why shifting from a consequence-based mindset focused on punishment will enable you to build bridges and foster connection.

Why consequences aren't effective

Let's explore why the consequence/punishment model doesn't work well for kids with FASD by examining the skills required for these approaches to be effective. As discussed in Chapter 4, common symptoms of FASD include deficits in impulse control, working memory, and executive functioning—all crucial for understanding and applying consequences.

Impulse control and decision-making

Impulse control is a primary skill needed for consequences to work. Neurotypical individuals often have the ability to pause, reflect, and weigh potential outcomes before acting. For example, when

I'm debating whether to eat more cookies, my brain goes through a rapid, subconscious process:

1. Acknowledging limits: *I've already had five cookies; that's enough.*
2. Weighing goals: *I'm trying to lose weight, and eating more cookies won't help.*
3. Rationalizing: *But I really want some chocolate chip cookies; maybe I miscounted how many I've already had.*
4. Justifying: *I took a long walk today, so I've earned it.*

This back-and-forth can take mere seconds, but it reflects a series of mental steps. Sometimes, I might resist the temptation and skip the cookie. Other times, I'll justify having another. Either way, my brain is functioning in a way that lets me evaluate my choices. I am able to weigh the options and make a decision.

For children and adolescents with FASD, this reflective process rarely occurs. Without strong impulse control, they may act on their immediate desires without any consideration of potential outcomes. A split-second decision—like grabbing a cookie, taking an object, or yelling at a teacher—happens before they even realize what they're doing.

The missing steps

When neurotypical individuals face a decision, their brains engage in processes like evaluating consequences, comparing past experiences, and predicting future outcomes. Kids with FASD often lack these abilities due to impairments in their brain function. Their actions are not a result of willful disobedience but of their brain's inability to pause and think through the situation.

This is why expecting consequences to work is unrealistic for individuals with FASD. Their brains don't naturally follow the step-by-step process needed to connect actions with outcomes, making it almost impossible for punishment to deter future behavior effectively. Instead of fostering learning, imposing consequences often increases frustration and anxiety for both the child and the caregiver.

Working memory and the ineffectiveness of consequences

Let's consider another example to highlight how working memory impacts the ability to learn from consequences. Imagine you're speeding on a highway where you received a ticket about a year ago. Here's the internal debate that might run through your head:

1. *I don't get caught every time I speed, so I'll probably be fine this time.*
2. *I really hate being late; speeding will help me make up time.*
3. *But if I get another ticket, my car insurance could go up.*
4. *I'm actually a safe driver, even when I speed.*
5. *This highway's speed limit is too low anyway.*

Even with a fully functional memory, your brain juggles these conflicting thoughts. Sometimes, the logical argument wins; other times, the emotional need to be on time takes over.

For someone with FASD, this process looks very different. Working-memory deficits mean that the details of past experiences—like the consequences of a previous speeding ticket—are less likely to be accessible in the moment. They may vaguely recall having been in trouble for speeding but won't connect that experience to their current situation.

If a person can't retain or access memories of past consequences, how can we expect them to use those consequences to guide future behavior?

The role of frustration and misunderstanding

I've worked with countless families struggling with this dynamic. One instance stands out vividly: I was in the living room with a husband and wife, explaining how their daughter's brain worked and why they were facing behavioral challenges. As I spoke, the father became visibly frustrated. He slammed his fist on the coffee table and exclaimed, "I REFUSE TO LOWER MY EXPECTATIONS!"

I calmly replied, "Good! We are not going to lower them; we are going to adjust them based on the child you are parenting. Would you expect a blind child to read a book that isn't in braille? No, of course not. Expecting your daughter, who has a hidden brain injury, to do things she is not capable of is the same thing. We are not lowering expectations; we are adjusting them based on her abilities."

This analogy seemed to resonate, and I could see the shift in the father's understanding. Adjusting expectations isn't about giving up or settling; it's about meeting the child where they are to set them up for success.

The bigger picture

When caregivers understand that their child's struggles stem from brain-based differences rather than intentional defiance, they can approach discipline and learning with more empathy and effectiveness. Instead of relying on consequences that don't stick, they can focus on strategies that build skills and strengthen relationships. In the next sections, we'll delve deeper into practical approaches that move beyond the punishment model.

When I talk to caregivers about moving away from consequences, one of the most common objections I hear is, "Don't they ever need to be held accountable?" This comes from a genuine place of wanting to teach responsibility and help their child improve behavior. The reality, however, is that if consequences aren't effective, continuing to use them is just spinning wheels. We're wasting time and energy without achieving the desired result.

Another frequent comment is, "But they're going to face consequences in the real world, so they need to understand them." This sentiment is rooted in fear—that if we don't prepare our children for real-world accountability, we're setting them up to fail.

Shifting the focus

Years ago, during an in-person support group, a caregiver raised this exact concern. She shared her frustration about her 19-year-old daughter's therapist. The therapist they'd been working with for years had started using a new approach, which the caregiver called "some kind of Heather Forbes, no consequences thing." She was referring to a book by Heather Forbes and Bryan Post, *Beyond Consequences, Logic, and Control*, which advocates for a connected, trauma-informed approach to parenting.[1]

This caregiver, who attended the group sporadically, was visibly upset. I had worked with this family before, attending Individualized Education Program (IEP) meetings and meeting privately with the parents, so I had some context for their journey.

I asked her a series of questions—not to challenge her but to guide her toward a new perspective and for the group members to learn.

First, I asked, "How long have you had your daughter?"

She replied, "Since birth. We got her right out of the hospital."

Next, I asked, "How long have you been giving her consequences?"

She said, "Probably since she was two."

Then, I asked the critical question, "Are they working?"

Her answer: "No."

This was the perfect opportunity to share my favorite quote again from Walter Barbe: "If you've told a child a thousand times and they still haven't learned, it is not the child who is the slow learner."

The caregiver was holding on to the idea that consequences

would eventually work if they just stayed consistent enough or found the "right" consequence. But after nearly two decades, it was clear that this approach wasn't helping her daughter. This is where the shift needs to happen—not in lowering expectations, but in adjusting strategies to meet the child where they were, developmentally and neurologically. These approaches had also greatly impacted their relationship. I had personally observed a strained relationship between the two caregivers and the young adult.

Caregivers often impose consequences on children, such as taking away a toy or canceling an activity when a child misbehaves. In addition to these imposed consequences, there are also natural consequences. For example, if a child breaks a toy, they no longer have it to play with, or if neighborhood children witness them hitting a sibling, they may not want to play with them.

Consequences are rooted in the assumption that the child has the cognitive ability to connect the dots between their actions and the resulting outcomes. For many individuals with FASD or trauma histories, this connection simply isn't there. Instead of teaching accountability, consequences often escalate anxiety, frustration, and feelings of failure—making it even harder for the child to learn.

When we understand this, we can focus on approaches that truly help our kids grow. These approaches don't ignore accountability: they redefine it in a way that aligns with how their brains work. Instead of rigid punishments, we teach through connection, relationship, and repetition, which ultimately fosters trust and learning in ways consequences cannot.

Whenever I hear someone say, "But they are going to face consequences in the real world, so they need to understand them," my response is always: "You're absolutely right. Our kids will likely face consequences in school, the justice system, relationships, or employment. But if they don't have a strong relationship with their family when they face those consequences, it will hurt them far more."

Why keep using what doesn't work?

If a strategy doesn't work for a particular child, why do we keep using it? Think about how we approach a crying baby. We don't keep changing their diaper over and over if they're still upset. We try different strategies—maybe they need a bottle, or to be rocked, or walked around. We instinctively adjust our approach to meet their needs until we find something that works.

Yet, for some reason, many of us—myself included—cling to consequences as a go-to parenting strategy, even when it consistently fails. My husband and I used consequence-based approaches for well over ten years. Sure, it may have worked in isolated instances, but it didn't work consistently.

Learning from lived experiences

When we finally let go of the consequence-based mindset, everything started to shift. We stopped focusing on punishment and started focusing on connection. We began asking:

- What does she need at this moment?
- How can we support her brain in a way that helps her regulate and learn?

The result? Our relationship with Akila improved, and her behaviors began to decrease. It wasn't magic, and it didn't happen overnight, but the shift from a punitive to a connected approach made all the difference.

For children with FASD, consequences in the form of punishments rarely teach what we hope they will. What truly helps is creating an environment where they feel safe, supported, and understood. When that foundation is in place, they're better equipped to face the challenges—and yes, the consequences—they will inevitably encounter in the real world.

When we keep using consequence-based strategies, the negative impacts can be profound. One of the most significant harms is to our children's self-esteem. While it may seem that they don't care when they're in trouble, the reality is that being constantly criticized, lectured, or reprimanded wears on them deeply. It doesn't feel good to be:

- constantly in trouble
- repeatedly lectured about their behavior
- hearing they are a disappointment
- labeled as "trouble"
- yelled at regularly.

Over time, this messaging becomes their internal narrative: *I am a problem. I am trouble. I disappoint everyone.* This internalized negativity can profoundly impact their self-worth and how they view themselves in the world.

Think about a time when you felt heavily criticized in your own life. Many people share stories about feeling as if they could never please their in-laws—especially their mother-in-law. It brings to mind Debra from the 1990s sitcom *Everybody Loves Raymond.* Debra's mother-in-law, Marie, constantly criticized her cooking and housekeeping, making her feel as if she could never win.

This same dynamic often plays out with our children, especially those with FASD. They feel as if they are always being scolded, lectured, or corrected and never celebrated for who they are.

Insights from adults with FASD

When I speak to adults living with FASD, they frequently share a common piece of advice for caregivers: "Focus on your relationship with your child. When I was growing up, I always felt as if I was in trouble, as if I was broken, and I didn't feel close to my parents. They were always trying to 'fix' me."

Hearing this from those who have lived it can be eye-opening. It underscores the importance of prioritizing connection over correction.

Regrets from experienced caregivers

Similarly, when I ask seasoned caregivers what they would do differently, many share a strikingly similar reflection: "I wish I had focused more on building a strong relationship with my child and spent less time trying to fix them with therapies, tutoring, medications, and interventions."

This isn't to say that interventions and therapies don't have a place—they absolutely do. But when they come at the expense of the caregiver–child relationship, the child often feels like a project instead of a person who is loved for who they are.

The role of therapy

It's not about ignoring challenges or giving up on helping children grow. It's about rethinking priorities. When we focus on strengthening the relationship and understanding the child's needs, we build a foundation where growth, learning, and connection can thrive. This shift can be transformative—not just for the child but for the entire family.

I'm not suggesting that traditional interventions shouldn't be attempted; many have their place. However, I've seen too many caregivers hyperfocus on trying to fix their children. Therapy can be a valuable tool, but we must be mindful not to overdo it. Many of our kids end up, in my opinion, over-therapized. (I know that's not a real word, but I use it all the time!) These children often spend much of their lives in therapy, with little noticeable improvement.

One of the most frequent questions I get from caregivers and professionals is: "What therapy should we have these kids in?" This is a complex question with no one-size-fits-all answer.

From my experience, occupational therapy tends to be the most effective intervention for individuals with FASD. Dr. Bruce Perry's Neurosequential Model of Therapeutics[2] provides valuable insight into this. He emphasizes that interventions should target the base of the brain first, working upward. Unfortunately, most therapies—such as dialectical behavior therapy (DBT), cognitive behavioral therapy (CBT), applied behavior analysis (ABA), multisystemic therapy (MST), attachment therapy, and other modalities—are top-down approaches. These require strong executive function skills, which are often underdeveloped in individuals with FASD.

From my experience, many families also explore interventions like gluten-/casein-free diets, neuro-biofeedback, brain mapping, brain spotting, Masgutova Neurosensorimotor Reflex Integration (MNRI), or other alternative therapies. While some families report minor improvements, the results are rarely transformative. Caregivers must weigh the benefits against the time, energy, financial commitment, and potential impact on the child's self-esteem.

My advice to families is to trust their instincts when making these decisions. No one knows your child better than you.

Improving the caregiver–child relationship

Another critical reason to move away from consequence-based strategies is their impact on the caregiver–child relationship. When we rely heavily on punishments and consequences, it can erode trust and connection.

I know a remarkable caregiver—a single mother to two children—whose story illustrates this point. Her daughter was diagnosed with FASD around age eight. At the time, their relationship was strained. Her daughter didn't say, "I love you," didn't trust her mom, and avoided spending time with her. This mom was using typical parenting strategies, which simply didn't work for her neurodivergent daughter.

Everything changed when the mom began learning about FASD and adopting connected relational parenting strategies. She shifted her focus from trying to "fix" her daughter to meeting her where she was. Over time, their relationship blossomed.

One day, this mother told me about a 6 a.m. photoshoot she set up in their backyard before her daughter left for school. A few years earlier, she would never have considered doing this during the busy morning routine. But embracing a connected philosophy brought out a new joy in her parenting journey.

This shift didn't just strengthen their relationship—it also changed how the mom viewed her role. Parenting became less about correcting her child's behaviors and more about building trust, connection, and shared moments of joy.

The takeaway is this—we can't "fix" our kids with FASD, nor should that be our goal. What we can do is meet them where they are, focus on connection, and create an environment where they feel safe, valued, and loved. The results may not always show up in traditional ways, but the strength of the relationship will be the foundation for their growth.

Connected/Relational supports

Dr. Karyn Purvis and Dr. David Cross developed Trust-Based Relational Intervention (TBRI),[3] a framework centered on connection, which has been widely adopted by the adoption, foster, and kinship care communities. One of the guiding principles of TBRI is the phrase: *Connection before correction.* This principle highlights the importance of building trust and relationship as the foundation for supporting children and adolescents, especially those with trauma or neurodivergence like FASD. I encourage anyone caring for a child with FASD to explore and learn more about TBRI, as its strategies are transformative for both caregivers and children.

Connection creates safety. It sends a message to the child that they are seen, heard, and valued—regardless of their behaviors. When we connect first, we calm their brain and body, which allows them to regulate and process emotions more effectively. From this state of regulation, learning and growth can occur.

Incorporating relational strategies like TBRI® and the insights from Dr. Delahooke into your parenting or professional work can make a world of difference. Instead of reacting to behaviors, you can respond with curiosity and compassion, creating an environment where children feel safe to grow and thrive.

Understanding neuro-behavioral challenges

To truly support children with FASD, we must shift our perspective from focusing on the behavior itself to understanding the brain-based reasons behind it. Dr. Mona Delahooke's books—*Beyond Behaviors: Using Brain Science and Compassion to Solve Children's Behavioral Challenges*[4] and *Brain–Body Parenting: How to Stop Managing Behavior and Start Raising Joyful, Resilient Kids*[5]—offer invaluable insights for caregivers. These books encourage adults to dig deeper into the root causes of behaviors rather than addressing them solely at the surface level.

One of my favorite quotes from Dr. Delahooke's *Beyond Behaviors* profoundly reframes how we view challenging behaviors:

> In paradigms that focus solely on behaviors, the question generally is: *What is the child getting out of the behavior?* (Attention? Control?) In this new paradigm, the question is different: *What are behaviors telling us about the child's underlying neurophysiological processes?* (Page 20)

This shift is critical, especially for children with FASD. Traditional behavior-based approaches often assume children act out intentionally—for attention, control, or manipulation. While this may sometimes be true because they are still kids, for children with FASD, the majority of their behaviors are symptoms of their brain injury and are most often rooted in anxiety.

Moving away from behavior-based paradigms

The behavior-focused paradigm dominates how most parents, teachers, and even therapists approach challenging behaviors. It's what many of us were taught to believe: behaviors are purposeful, and children just need to be corrected or disciplined to "fix" them. However, this approach can unintentionally harm children with FASD, whose actions are frequently driven by brain-based challenges like impulsivity, difficulty processing sensory input, or fear.

Understanding the neuro-behavioral root of these actions allows us to approach children with compassion. Rather than asking, "How do I stop this behavior?" we can ask, "What is this behavior telling me about what this child needs?"

FASD and anxiety

Anxiety is a significant driver of behaviors for individuals with FASD. Because of their neurodevelopmental challenges, children with FASD often face:

- difficulty understanding and predicting the world around them
- challenges processing sensory information or changes in routines
- frustration over unmet expectations or communication struggles.

When these anxieties build, behaviors emerge—not as a means to manipulate or control, but as a child's way of expressing an unmet need or coping with overwhelming emotions.

The role of anxiety and trauma in behavior

It's critical to understand the neurobiology of anxiety. I shared some information about anxiety in Chapter 4. When I lived in Minnesota for 52 years, I drove through countless snow and ice storms. Sometimes it took three or four times as long to reach my destination because of the slick roads. By the time I arrived, I would often have an aching lower back from the tension and stress of the drive.

Now, imagine a child experiencing that same level of tension and anxiety—not just during one isolated event, but regularly; for some kids, it is during each waking moment. When our children are feeling anxious, their brains are "on fire."

- Do you think they can listen effectively at that moment?
- Are they able to process and apply what we're trying to teach them?
- Do they feel connected to us?

In most cases, the answer is no. Instead of focusing on what may be coming out of their mouth—be it disrespectful words, yelling, or avoidance—we need to dig deeper. We need to identify the source of their anxiety. What has made them stressed and anxious? That's the key to truly supporting them. If your adolescent is coming home after curfew, nothing you say to them when they get home is likely to have an impact, because they walk in through the door with their brain on fire. Wait until the next day.

Consequences and trauma

One of the most significant shifts in our parenting approach came when we realized that traditional consequences were not only ineffective for Akila but were adding trauma to her life. For example, when we threw away her blankie at age six because she was stealing, we caused her emotional trauma.

At the time, we acted with the best intentions. We believed that taking away something she loved would teach her not to steal. But we acted on the wrong information and lacked understanding of the brain-based reasons behind her behavior. Now, we deeply regret throwing away her blankie. We've apologized to Akila many times over the years, and she always forgives us. Still, it was a turning point in our parenting.

Other caregivers, sometimes out of desperation, have gone further than throwing away a beloved item. Some use shaming language or emotionally abusive tactics, believing harsh words will change behavior. Others turn to physical punishment.

I am begging you not to take this approach. It not only fails to address the root cause of the behavior but also inflicts further harm on a child who is already struggling with a hidden disability. In the past decade, I've become deeply interested in understanding how trauma and the brain intersect. What I've learned has only strengthened my belief in avoiding physical punishment entirely. Research, such as the study by Cuartas *et al.* (2021),[6] shows that spanking alters children's brain responses in ways similar to extreme maltreatment. This reinforces the need to parent with empathy and connection, especially for children with unique challenges like FASD.

Key points of connected relational parenting

1. **Focus on the relationship:**
    - Even in the toughest moments with big behaviors, ask yourself: *How can I connect with my child right now?*
    - When Akila starts to get upset, I often try to redirect her energy by revisiting positive memories, singing songs from her childhood, or inviting her to do something

with me. It doesn't always work, but it's always worth trying.

2. **Avoid shaming language:**
   - Shame erodes connection and trust. It tells the child, "You are the problem," instead of "This behavior is a challenge we can work through together." Unfortunately, many of us fall into the habit of using shame-based language without even realizing it.
   - Here are some examples of shaming phrases to avoid:
     - "You should know better."
     - "Act your age."
     - "What were you thinking?"
     - "You always forget your phone."
     - "You're acting like a baby."
     - "Why can't you be more like [someone else]?"
     - "Stop making a scene."
     - "Didn't you learn the first time?"
     - "Use your brain."
   - These phrases not only hurt the child but also set the stage for a negative self-narrative:
     - "I'm a bad person."
     - "I can't do anything right."
     - "I'll never be enough."

3. **Replace shame with connection and support:**
   - Instead of defaulting to shame-based reactions, consider shifting your approach.
   - Replace "You should know better" with "It looks like this is really hard for you. Let's work through it together."
   - Swap "Why can't you be more like [someone else]?" with "I see how hard you're trying. Let's figure out what's going on here."

- Change "Stop crying" to "It's okay to feel upset. I'm here to help you."

When we avoid shame and focus on connection, we create an environment where children feel safe and supported.

Using connected relational strategies takes time, practice, and self-awareness. It's not about being a perfect parent—it's about creating an environment where your child knows you're on their team, even in the hard moments. Shame, whether it's subtle or overt, only deepens the divide between caregiver and child. By consciously replacing shaming language with compassionate communication, we foster trust, understanding, and ultimately, healing.

The goal isn't to raise perfect kids—it's to raise kids who feel loved, supported, and connected, even when they're struggling.

Responding to behaviors with empathy

Think back to a time when you made a mistake at work or upset someone important to you. Your anxiety likely skyrocketed—you couldn't sleep, couldn't think clearly, and maybe even became short-tempered or defensive. Now imagine the compounding effect this has on a child or adolescent, especially one with a brain injury like FASD.

When shame enters the picture, the child goes into survival mode. Their brain interprets the situation as a threat, making it impossible for them to focus on learning, problem-solving, or emotional regulation.

Let's take the example of a child breaking an electronic device, such as an iPad. A common (but unhelpful) response is, "Well, you broke it, so now you'll have to live without it."

This response, while logical, doesn't take into account the

neurobehavioral realities of a child with FASD. Instead, it reinforces feelings of shame and defensiveness.

A more effective response is, "Oh bummer, the iPad broke. It's going to take some time to fix it, so we'll need to find other activities in the meantime." A response like this, in the moment, is going to be more effective.

When revisiting the situation later, the emphasis should be on teaching responsibility rather than punishment. This distinction is critical for children with FASD:

1. **Timing is key:** Wait a day or two, until you find the child is calm and in a "good brain place," meaning they are emotionally regulated and able to engage in a constructive conversation.

2. **Use clear and simple language:** Avoid complex reasoning or abstract concepts such as, "This is what happens when...." Instead, focus on concrete actions, such as, "We need to fix the iPad, and that takes money. Let's work together to find a way to help."

3. **Frame responsibility positively:** Instead of saying, "You need to pay for what you broke," say, "We can do some extra chores to help fix the iPad. Let's make a plan together."

4. **Reinforce success:** Celebrate small steps toward problem-solving. For example, "You did a great job helping with those chores today. We're getting closer to fixing the iPad!"

This approach is empathetic, avoids blame, and focuses on problem-solving rather than punishment. It doesn't mean the child or adolescent isn't going to be upset about the iPad and perseverate on it, but this approach is still better than the first response.

The role of professionals

Unfortunately, shame doesn't just come from caregivers; it often comes from professionals like teachers, therapists, or crisis workers.

- A mental-health crisis worker saying to a child, "Come out here and talk to me or you'll hurt my feelings," may think they're being relatable, but this approach is guilt-inducing and unlikely to build trust.
- Educators may inadvertently escalate situations by crowding a dysregulated child, drawing attention to their behavior, or pressuring them to respond before they feel safe.

A case example: De-escalation in a school setting

I was called to help with a fifth-grade girl with FASD who was having a meltdown in a school office at the school my children attended. She was under a desk, crying and yelling, surrounded by several staff who were in the office with her, and several other staff were observing through a window, but still visible to her. The situation was unintentionally overwhelming for the child and escalated her dysregulation. These are the steps I took:

1. **Reduced overstimulation:** I turned off the fluorescent lights in the room to minimize sensory overload.
2. **Limited the audience:** I asked most of the staff to leave the room and the hallway to reduce the child's anxiety and the feeling of being watched.
3. **Respected personal space:** I sat quietly on the floor, far

enough away to avoid crowding her but close enough to signal my presence.

4. **Talked little:** In order to allow their brain to slow down, we should be quiet.

5. **Used connection, not correction:** Once she began to calm, I gently asked about a topic I knew she loved—her pets. This shifted her focus away from her dysregulated state and onto something that made her feel safe and happy.

After about 15 minutes of talking about her pets, she was calm enough to take a walk with me, providing further sensory regulation.

After this incident, I debriefed with the school principal and staff about the importance of reducing sensory overload, respecting personal space, and avoiding behaviors that escalate a situation. The staff were receptive, and I later provided training to help them better support students with FASD and trauma histories.

Key takeaways

1. **Shame escalates; empathy de-escalates:** Avoid language or actions that make a child feel judged, embarrassed, or blamed.

2. **Reduce sensory triggers:** Minimize noise, light, and crowds during moments of dysregulation.

3. **Respect personal space:** Trauma histories make physical proximity critical—don't crowd or hover.

4. **Focus on connection:** Use topics of interest, soft tones, and body language that convey safety.

5. **Stop talking:** We need to allow them to slow their brain down, which they can't do while processing our words.

6. **Be patient:** Regulation takes time. Don't rush or demand immediate compliance.

The goal is not to "fix" the behavior in the moment but to help the child feel safe and supported so they can regulate and move forward. When we know better, we do better.

Chapter 6

Using Connected Relational Strategies with Developmentally Scattered Profiles

In this chapter, we explore strategies and approaches that align with the unique needs of individuals with fetal alcohol spectrum disorder (FASD), helping to foster connection, understanding, and more effective support.

Developmentally scattered profiles

Children with FASD often exhibit a developmentally scattered profile, meaning their functional abilities vary significantly across different areas of development and situations. For example, a child may be chronologically ten years old, but their functional age could align closer to that of a five-year-old.

A general guideline often used for children with FASD is to take their chronological age and cut it in half to estimate their developmental functioning. This adjustment is not a strict rule but can give caregivers and professionals a starting point for setting realistic expectations. For example:

- A 10-year-old may function, on average, more like a five-year-old.
- A 16-year-old may have the emotional regulation skills of an eight-year-old.

Inconsistent abilities

The scattered profile of a child with FASD means their abilities can fluctuate dramatically depending on the situation, environment, and emotional state. For example, in one moment, a ten-year-old child may seem to function like a two-year-old, struggling with emotional outbursts or impulsivity. A few minutes later, they might surprise you by showing the maturity or insight of a 12-year-old, especially if it's an area of personal interest or strength.

By adapting to their developmentally scattered profile, we can create environments that better support their growth, regulation, and well-being. Below is an example of a developmentally scattered profile of an 18-year-old:

Actual age: 18

Skill	Developmental age equivalent
Expressive language	20
Comprehension	6
Money and time concepts	8
Emotional maturity	6
Physical maturity	18
Reading ability	16
Social skills	7
Living skills	11

Adapted from the research findings of Streissguth, Clarren *et al.*, & Diane Malbin, Trying Differently Rather Than Harder.

Developmental profile and the neurobehavioral model

This developmental profile, grounded in Diane Malbin's neurobehavioral model,[1] provides insight into the functional differences in children and adolescents with FASD, especially those with IQs above 70 (the cut-off for intellectual disability). While this framework won't perfectly fit every individual, it gives a strong starting point for understanding the unique challenges and strengths associated with FASD.

One of the hallmark features of this developmental profile is the discrepancy between expressive language skills and emotional or cognitive development:

- At age 18, many individuals with FASD have expressive language skills that exceed their chronological age (e.g. comparable to a 20-year-old).
- However, their emotional maturity and comprehension may align with that of a six-year-old.

This gap creates significant confusion for caregivers, educators, therapists, and others who interact with the individual. Because they sound neurotypical, their behaviors often appear willful and intentional to adults who are unaware of their underlying brain differences.

"Masking" and misunderstanding

Due to their strong verbal abilities, children and adolescents with FASD often "pass" as neurotypical in short-term or surface-level interactions. This can confuse professionals, as doctors, therapists, and social workers who spend limited time with the individual may not recognize the developmental gaps, leading to misdiagnoses or inappropriate interventions.

It can also create dilemmas at school. Many children with FASD display few behaviors at school but unleash emotional dysregulation at home, leaving caregivers struggling to convince professionals of the full extent of the challenges. For many of our kids, by the time they are in secondary school, they start to struggle more behaviorally and academically.

My friend Jeff Noble, an FASD educator, often references the Tom Hanks movie *Big* to illustrate this developmental gap. In the film, Tom Hanks's character is a 12-year-old boy in an adult's body, navigating adult situations with childlike reactions. Examples include the character standing through a limousine moonroof, repeatedly pushing buttons, and spitting out caviar at a party and putting it back on the tray—all typical behaviors for a child but jarring and inappropriate for an adult.

When teens or adults with FASD exhibit behaviors that don't match their chronological age, they are frequently judged harshly. A 6-year-old's tantrum may be tolerated, but a 16-year-old's tantrum is often seen as defiant or manipulative. Behaviors that are developmentally typical for their emotional age are viewed as bizarre or immature by those unaware of their FASD.

Adulting with a scattered developmental profile

For an 18-year-old with the emotional maturity of a 6-year-old, "adulting" becomes extraordinarily challenging. Tasks like managing relationships, employment, or independent living become overwhelming when their developmental capacity doesn't match societal expectations.

This gap doesn't just affect the individual—it places immense strain on families, educators, and professionals. Recognizing the developmentally scattered profile is the first step toward providing appropriate supports and reducing shame and frustration for everyone involved.

I often say that for children and adolescents with FASD, it's as if their brains "get stuck" in a toddler-like state during moments of stress or anxiety. While they may function at higher levels in certain aspects of their lives, when their brains "go on fire," many revert to toddler-like responses until they approach somewhere around 30 years old.

This toddler-like reaction isn't consistent across all areas of life but is particularly evident in moments of dysregulation, stress, or transition. For example, they may struggle with decision-making, emotional regulation, and impulse control, just as a toddler would. This reversion makes high-pressure situations—like living on their own, attending university, or working in a fast-paced environment—exceptionally difficult.

Post-secondary education and employment realities

When we look at the developmental timeline of an 18-year-old with FASD, we see the challenges clearly. Their chronological age might qualify them for higher education or employment, but their developmental functioning could align closer to a six- or eight-year-old in areas like executive functioning, emotional regulation, and impulse control.

This gap raises important points:

1. **University or post-secondary education:**
    - How do we expect them to navigate schedules, deadlines, and independence without significant supports in place?
    - Many will struggle with understanding expectations, organizing their time, or advocating for help when needed.

2. **Work in the community:**
   - In a grocery store, for example, they might excel at concrete, repetitive tasks but struggle with customer service, managing mistakes, running a cash register, or adapting to unexpected changes.
   - Without accommodations or patient employers, they may face frequent criticism or job loss, further damaging their self-esteem.

Unrealistic expectations after high school

I often say to schools and families, "If it took extraordinary efforts by the school and family to get this student through high school, what makes you think they will suddenly succeed in more schooling or employment right after graduation?" This is unrealistic and often sets up the young adult—and their family—for failure. We need to shift this mindset and create pathways that allow for gradual, supported transitions into adulthood.

Traditionally, school transition programs were developed for individuals with visible disabilities. FASD, as a hidden brain injury, requires a different approach. Unfortunately, many systems aren't designed to meet the needs of individuals with FASD, leaving them underserved.

A common experience: Flourishing in their thirties

In several FASD podcasts and my own conversations with adults living with FASD, a recurring theme emerges: Many say that their thirties were when they started to feel that they functioned better.

By age 30, the developmental profile of someone with FASD might resemble that of a 15-year-old, which aligns with when neurotypical individuals begin to gain more maturity and responsibility. By this age, their brain has often developed enough to improve emotional regulation, decision-making, and executive functioning to a degree.

Caregivers who understand this timeline are better able to set realistic expectations and create long-term plans that prioritize safety, growth, and connection rather than rushing independence too soon.

Interdependence

In our work with FASD individuals and their families, my fellow coaches and I actively avoid using the term "independence." Instead, we emphasize the concept of "interdependence." This is not just a matter of semantics—it reflects a fundamental truth about how all of us, regardless of our abilities, function in the world. None of us is truly independent; we all rely on others and various tools to help us navigate life and reach our full potential.

For example, if my phone didn't remind me to take my medications each evening, I would likely forget. I depend on my husband for emotional support and shared responsibilities. My doctor, therapist, hair stylist, boss, and countless others play roles in helping me function effectively in the world. This web of support doesn't make me less capable—it allows me to focus my energy on the things I do best while leaning on others where I need help.

For children and adults with FASD, this concept is even more critical. These individuals often have very concrete ways of thinking, which makes the abstract idea of interdependence harder to grasp. Many of them grow up believing that turning 18 or 21 is a magical transformation into adulthood, where they can suddenly manage everything on their own. They may think that adulthood means complete freedom and autonomy, without the need for guidance or support. This belief sets them up for frustration, confusion, and failure when reality doesn't match their expectations.

We need to normalize the idea that everyone has a "team" of supporters—people and systems working behind the scenes to help them succeed. A powerful way to make this concept concrete is by using examples from their own world. Let's consider a professional athlete, for instance. This is someone many young people idolize. They see an NBA or WNBA basketball player scoring points, performing incredible feats, and receiving accolades on the court. What they don't see is the extensive team behind the scenes making that success possible.

We can break it down for them:

- The agent negotiates contracts and manages press releases.
- The coach provides daily guidance and strategic advice to improve their game.
- The nutritionist designs meal plans to keep them in peak physical condition.
- The assistant schedules appointments and maintains their calendar.
- The financial advisor handles their money to ensure they have financial stability.

The athlete may be the one on the court, but their performance is only possible because of the support system surrounding them. This analogy can be an eye-opener for young people with FASD, who might otherwise believe that success comes from individual effort alone.

To help our kids truly understand interdependence, we must start these conversations early. Use visuals to make the concept tangible—create a "team chart" for them. This could include family members, teachers, therapists, friends, and even tools like apps or visual schedules that help them function. By making interdependence a natural and normalized concept in their minds, we can set them up to embrace the support they need as they grow.

We also need to make this a part of everyday language. When we drop the term "independence" and replace it with "interdependence," we reduce the pressure they feel to live up to an unrealistic standard of self-sufficiency. At the same time, we open up the possibility for them to see asking for help and relying on others as a strength, not a weakness.

When we focus on building interdependence instead of striving for an unattainable independence, we empower individuals with FASD to thrive in a way that feels natural, supported, and achievable.

The developmental quadrant: A tool for understanding scattered development

One of the most effective tools I've encountered in my work with families and professionals is the *developmental quadrant*. This tool helps us visualize and understand where an individual functions developmentally across various areas, rather than focusing solely on their chronological age. I was introduced to it in 2016 by Kim Stevens, an incredible mentor I met while working at Families Rising. Kim's expertise and guidance have been invaluable, and this quadrant is one of the many tools she taught me that I now use regularly.

The developmental quadrant is especially helpful in cases where an individual's abilities are developmentally scattered—a common characteristic of individuals with FASD and other neurodevelopmental conditions. It allows caregivers, teachers, and professionals to see where a child or young adult might excel in one area but need significant support in another. This clearer understanding often leads to better, more targeted strategies.

Case example: A high school student

I used this tool in an Individualized Education Program (IEP) meeting for a 16-year-old high school student who was frequently getting into trouble during hallway passing times. The school had been suspending him for his behavior, assuming he could control it because he didn't engage in it every day. Their reasoning was that since he could behave "appropriately" at times, he simply needed to make better choices. This is a typical misunderstanding, as behaviors in children with FASD often look willful, even when they are not.

The student's parents had been asking for supervision during passing times, explaining that their son needed support to navigate these unstructured moments. The school, however, pushed back, claiming that providing additional support would be enabling him. They believed he just needed to "try harder." This mindset is all too common in schools and underscores the need for tools like the developmental quadrant to bridge the gap in understanding.

During the IEP meeting, I stood up, walked to the whiteboard, and drew a simple chart with horizontal and vertical lines to form four quadrants. I labeled the top-left quadrant with his chronological age: 16 years old. From there, I began filling in the other quadrants to represent his developmental levels in different areas.

In the top-right quadrant of the developmental quadrant, we delve into the individual's emotional age—a critical aspect when understanding and supporting children or young adults with scattered developmental profiles. Emotional age often determines how someone responds to various situations, and influences their ability to self-regulate and interact socially. While chronological age sets societal expectations, emotional age provides a clearer picture of the person's developmental reality.

During the IEP meeting for the 16-year-old student, I posed a series of questions to the team to help assess his emotional age. These questions were designed to uncover patterns in his reactions and interests, comparing them to those of a neurotypical teenager of the same age.

1. How does he respond to things when he is really excited or happy about something? Is it similar to how a neurotypical 16-year-old would respond?

2. How does he respond to something when he is upset, frustrated, or angry? Is it similar to how a neurotypical 16-year-old would respond?

3. How does he respond when he is sick, hurt, or injured? Is it similar to how a neurotypical 16-year-old would respond?

4. What type of TV shows, movies, video games, and outdoor activities does he like to do? Is it what we would see a neurotypical 16-year-old being interested in?

As the parents and school staff talked about this, they decided he was functioning emotionally as a five-year-old.

In the bottom-left quadrant, we try to figure out their social age. The question I asked the team was: Does he hang out with neurotypical 16-year-olds? The answer was no, he hung out with other neurodivergent students who functioned similarly to how he did. So I asked his parents if there was an age group they noticed him gravitating toward when he was playing in their neighborhood or at family events. They said his seven- to eight-year-old cousins were who he enjoyed hanging out with the most. We put seven down as his social age.

In the bottom-right quadrant, we put down their cognitive age. For this, we can look at where they are grading at on standardized tests. He was at about a nine-year-old cognitively.

Developmental quadrant

Physical/chronological age	Emotional age
	Support/connect/relate to this age
Social age	**Cognitive age**
Provide support and guidance with and about peers and safety measures	Advocate at school regarding this age

Outcome of the meeting

This tool shifted the conversation from blaming the student for his actions to understanding his needs. The team recognized that his emotional immaturity and cognitive limitations made unsupervised passing time too challenging for him. As we were doing this developmental quadrant with the school team, the coordinator of special education had an epiphany. He said that he had eight-year-old twins and he would never let them wander the hallways of the high school unsupervised. The school started to provide supervision for this young man during hallway passing time.

Instead of expecting him to "behave better," the IEP team adjusted their approach by:

- providing supervision during hallway passing times
- adjusting expectations to align with his developmental ages
- developing strategies that met him where he was, rather than where his chronological age suggested he should be.

This approach aligns with connected relational strategies and fosters an environment where the child can feel understood and supported, not judged or penalized for limitations beyond their control.

After we finished filling out this developmental quadrant, I took a moment to emphasize the importance of each quadrant and how it guides our approach to supporting individuals like this student. Understanding these developmental gaps allows us to tailor interventions and expectations to truly meet their needs rather than setting them up for failure.

Emotional age: The key to connection

I explained to the team that emotional age is the foundation we use to connect with an individual. With my own daughter, Akila, her emotional age has always been younger than her chronological age. Even now, at age 25, she loves jokes and humor that align with the developmental range of a four- to ten-year-old. For example, she loves silly puns and playful banter that might seem juvenile to some, but for her are pure joy.

My husband, Michael, has a knack for leaning into this emotional connection. He often tells her these light-hearted jokes, and she absolutely lights up. It's become a ritual that deepens their bond.

On my end, Akila gave me the nickname "Bertha" years ago, and I call her "Agnus" in return. This playful interaction is something we've maintained for years, even though my other young-adult kids find it quirky or odd. For Akila and me, though, it's a way to build attachment and create moments of shared joy that strengthen our relationship.

Emotional age isn't just about how someone processes feelings—it's also about how they connect. Understanding this helps us find creative ways to meet them where they are and build trust, attachment, and positive relationships.

Social age: Peers and safety

Next, I discussed how social age comes into play when making decisions about peer interactions and safety measures. It's one of the most critical areas for ensuring that these children feel supported and are kept safe in environments that match their developmental abilities.

With the example of the 16-year-old student, I asked the team to reflect on how his social age of seven might impact his ability to handle certain situations. Specifically:

- How would he do with a smartphone providing 24/7 access to the internet?
- Would we leave him home alone all day without supervision?
- Would we drop him off at a mall all day to hang out with friends?

The answer was clear—these would not be good ideas.

I related this to my experiences with Akila. When she was younger, we didn't fully understand the significance of her social and emotional developmental gaps. We often shamed her for making poor decisions on devices like smartphones, computers, or tablets. When she behaved inappropriately online—despite promising not to—we labeled her as "untrustworthy" or even a "liar." We didn't realize that we were setting her up for failure. Giving her access to these devices was essentially like handing a toddler the keys to the entire internet and expecting them to navigate it responsibly.

We tried safety programs and monitoring apps, but Akila would consistently find ways to bypass them. At the time, we didn't connect the dots between her apparent age-appropriate expressive language skills and her lower developmental profile. She *seemed* so typical for her age, but her actions reflected her actual social and emotional development, not her chronological age.

When we understand a child's social age, we can make safer and more supportive decisions, like structuring their time and providing appropriate supervision. It's also an opportunity to advocate for them in environments where their behaviors might be misunderstood, such as at school or in public spaces.

Cognitive age: Advocating in the school system

Finally, we talked about cognitive age and its role in advocating for the right accommodations and modifications within the school system. Many of our children and adolescents have average or even high IQs but struggle academically due to underlying challenges like comprehension difficulties, rigidity, or executive functioning deficits. Schools often focus solely on IQ and their expressive language abilities, which can lead to misplaced expectations and inappropriate support plans.

This is where a deep understanding of their cognitive developmental profile is essential. For example, a student might struggle with reading comprehension even if they can decode words fluently. They may become "stuck" on a particular task due to rigidity or an inability to shift their thinking. Executive functioning challenges, like planning or organizing tasks, can make academic success feel out of reach.

I explained how a lower social and emotional age compounds these struggles. Imagine trying to navigate a classroom environment where you're emotionally processing as a seven-year-old and socially functioning at the same level, but the academic and behavioral expectations are set for a 16-year-old. It's a recipe for frustration, failure, and often, disciplinary actions that don't address the root cause.

Compassion through understanding

I have highlighted a critical point: acknowledging how unfair this is for our kids. For years, Michael and I unintentionally shamed Akila for behaviors that stemmed from her developmental differences. When we expected her to act her chronological age without recognizing her scattered developmental profile, we set her up for failure—and then punished her for it.

Now, I encourage caregivers and educators to shift their mindset. Instead of focusing on what the child "should" be able to do, focus on what they can do and scaffold their environment accordingly. This requires compassion, patience, and a willingness to see the child's true developmental needs, not just their chronological age.

Understanding and using the developmental quadrant as a tool isn't just helpful—it's transformative. It allows us to meet children where they are, support them with appropriate resources, and ultimately help them thrive. By focusing on emotional connection, social safety, and cognitive support, we can create a world where these kids feel understood, empowered, and capable of achieving their potential.

"Expectation is the root of all heartache" (William Shakespeare)

Let's dive deeper into the idea of expectations. When caregivers or professionals set expectations that don't align with a child's developmental profile, the result is often frustration, disappointment, and a feeling of failure for both parties. This misalignment creates a cycle that is hard to break, especially when the child is blamed for their inability to meet expectations they aren't developmentally equipped to handle.

For instance, if you expect a child with executive functioning deficits to clean their room independently, you're likely to end up feeling frustrated when they can't follow through. And even if they managed to clean their room successfully a few months ago, that doesn't mean they can repeat the task today, especially if their brain is overwhelmed, their anxiety is high, or their environment has changed.

Unspoken expectations lead to resentment

American journalist and author Neil Strauss captures this perfectly in his quote: "Unspoken expectations are premeditated resentments."

I see this dynamic play out constantly in families. Caregivers often feel disappointed and hurt when children don't live up to unspoken expectations. For example, a caregiver might think, "They're ten years old; they should be able to do this without me." When the child doesn't meet that expectation, frustration builds.

One common area where mismatched expectations arise is with chores. Caregivers often ask:

- *Should I never expect them to help with anything?*
- *Does this mean they can't have any responsibilities?*

The answer is nuanced. It's absolutely okay to ask your child to help with chores, but you have to be flexible. Not every child will be able to contribute consistently, and even for those who can, there will be moments when they simply cannot cope. For example:

- Some children may be able to help with small, structured tasks regularly, like setting the table or sorting laundry.

- Others may only be able to assist sporadically, when their anxiety is low and they're in a good brain space.

- Some children may not be able to help at all, especially if they are already overwhelmed or rigidly focused on another activity.

- Many of them will be more successful if you partner with them on the chores and do it alongside them.

Knowing when to let go

Caregivers need to develop the skill of knowing when to let go. There will be moments when your child is simply unable to follow through with a task, no matter how small or simple it seems.

Examples of when letting go may be necessary:

1. **When anxiety is high:** If your child is feeling overwhelmed, pushing them to complete a chore may escalate their stress and lead to dysregulation.

2. **When they're hyperfocused:** Kids with FASD often have rigid thinking and struggle to shift gears. If they're deeply immersed in a video game or activity, stopping to complete a chore may be too much to ask in the moment.

3. **When it's a bad day:** Some days, their brain simply isn't firing in a way that allows for task completion.

Letting go doesn't mean you're giving up or being permissive. It means you're recognizing their limitations in the moment and prioritizing connection and emotional safety over compliance.

Strategies for success

- **Break down tasks:** Instead of asking your child to clean their entire room, break it down into smaller steps. For example, ask them to put all the toys in a bin first, then take a break before moving on to the next step.

- **Make it fun:** Turn chores into a game, like racing to see who can finish first or setting a timer for short bursts of cleaning.

- **Provide structure:** Use visual aids, checklists, or reminders to guide them through tasks.

- **Offer choices:** Instead of demanding, "Clean your room now," ask, "Would you like to clean your room after lunch or after your show?" This gives them some control while still meeting your goal.

- **Validate their feelings:** If they're resistant or upset, acknowledge their emotions: "I know it's hard to stop what you're doing right now. I'll help you get started so it feels easier."

Adjusting expectations

It's important to understand that adjusting your expectations is not the same as giving up on your child. Instead, it's about changing your approach to match their developmental profile and needs. By doing so, you'll create a more harmonious household where your child feels supported rather than criticized, and you'll reduce the stress and resentment that unspoken expectations can create.

Let's give ourselves permission to let go of what doesn't serve us—or our kids—and focus on what works.

Shove the sticker charts you know where

In Akila's early elementary years, we would sit in IEP meetings or talk with her teachers, who would tell us what a wonderful, hard-working, and compliant student she was. Meanwhile, at home, we were dealing with enormous challenges: verbal and physical aggression, intense anxiety, and constant dysregulation. My husband and I often felt as if we were losing our minds. Were we doing something wrong? Why was our daughter thriving at school but struggling so deeply at home?

Teachers, therapists, and doctors all weighed in with their advice, but the most common suggestion was token economy systems. For anyone unfamiliar, these involve using "tokens," like stickers, as rewards when children meet targeted behaviors. While widely used in schools and therapeutic settings, many caregivers of children with FASD—myself included—will tell you that sticker charts simply do not work for most of our kids.

The sticker chart dilemma

One time, I attended a professional conference on FASD with a panel of psychologists and experts. During the Q&A, another caregiver who was also a professional raised her hand and asked the exact question I was planning to ask: "But what do we do about the physical aggression?"

One of the psychologists I respected responded, "Use a jar and put a marble in it for every good behavior or when they respond appropriately."

I couldn't help myself. My hand shot up, and I blurted out, "A little bit of vomit comes up in my throat every time a professional suggests using the token economy with FASD because it rarely works."

The room went silent. People turned to look at me. I quickly apologized, admitting my frustration but reiterating that this strategy had been completely ineffective for our daughter. At the time, I didn't fully understand why sticker charts didn't work, but I knew from experience that they didn't.

Years later, I had the opportunity to co-train on FASD with that same psychologist. During our prep session, I brought up the incident and apologized for my outburst. He surprised me with his response: "That was you? I remember that moment. It made me really think deeply about token economy systems and why they don't work for kids with FASD. When I looked at the brain domains needed for it to succeed, it was clear it wouldn't be effective. I'm glad you challenged me."

Hearing this humbled me and deepened my respect for him. The best professionals aren't the ones who act as if they have all the answers—they're the ones willing to learn and grow.

Why token economies don't work for FASD

There are several reasons why sticker charts and similar reward systems fail for most kids with FASD:

1. **Impact on the brain's reward system:** Many individuals with FASD have disrupted reward systems in their brains due to early trauma and alcohol exposure. This makes it difficult for them to connect the dots between earning a reward and modifying their behavior.

2. **Time blindness:** Kids with FASD often struggle with understanding the concept of time. While they may be able to read a clock, they don't always *feel* the passage of time the way neurotypical individuals do. The promise of a prize "later"

or "at the end of the week" can feel like an eternity to them, making it ineffective as motivation.

3. **Abstract thinking challenges:** The abstract concept of earning and saving for a reward can be confusing. Even when kids understand the system, they may perseverate (obsess) over the prizes, leading to increased anxiety rather than improved behavior.

When Akila was in ninth grade, she attended a special education school where the first classroom she was placed in used a token economy system. Students earned points for good behavior, tracked them in checkbook registers, and could spend them on prizes every two weeks.

Within a week, Akila's anxiety had skyrocketed. She became hyperfocused on earning points and obsessed over what she could buy. The school quickly realized this approach wasn't working and moved her to a different program within the building.

The takeaway

If token economies work for your child, that's fantastic—keep using them. But if they don't, it's okay to ditch them entirely. FASD requires a different approach, one rooted in connection, understanding, and flexibility. Instead of trying to fit our kids into a system that doesn't work for them, let's build systems that meet their unique needs.

Sticker charts might work for some kids, but for many with FASD, they're just one more source of frustration—for everyone involved. So, to all the professionals who suggest them without understanding the brain behind the behavior: Maybe reconsider, and let's shove those sticker charts where they belong.

The thermostat

This story demonstrates how crucial connected and trauma-informed approaches are when working with individuals with FASD. Here's a breakdown of what happened one morning in Akila's group home, what could have been done differently, and why the alternative approach might have worked better:

What happened

- Akila woke up feeling overheated, a physical discomfort that likely heightened her anxiety and dysregulation and put her into sensory overload.
- She noticed that the thermostat was set higher than normal and became upset.
- The staff attempted to explain the situation logically, using abstract reasoning (temperature regulation in different levels of the home) that Akila's brain, under stress, was not equipped to process.
- Akila escalated, leading to an aggressive outburst and a series of traumatic events for her, the staff, and everyone involved. The police and ambulance were called and she spent the entire day in the emergency department. Thousands of dollars were wasted.

When the group home manager called me to update me on the situation, I asked how he coached the staff to handle the situation differently next time. He had no idea what I was talking about. So I told him how the staff should have responded differently, as is explained below.

What could have been done differently?

Staff could have:

- **acknowledged Akila's feelings immediately**—instead of explaining the thermostat setting, the could have validated her discomfort: "Oh no, you must be miserable, it is really hot!"

- **focused on solutions, not explanations**—offered a practical, calming response: "Let's adjust the thermostat right now and get it cooler in here. If it does not cool off within an hour or two, we may need to call the maintenance person."

- **provided immediate support for the physical discomfort**—offered her cold water, a fan, an ice pack, or a shower to help regulate her body and emotions: "While it cools down, let's figure out what would help you feel better right now. What do you think—an ice-cold drink, or maybe some time in front of a fan?"

- **kept the interaction relational**—used a tone of care and collaboration to de-escalate: "I have been hot all morning and I didn't think of looking at the thermostat: thank you! I want to help you feel comfortable as soon as possible."

This approach would have prioritized empathy and problem-solving, while also giving Akila the sense that her concerns were valid and that she had control over the situation. By focusing on meeting her immediate needs rather than defending or explaining the situation, it likely would have diffused her frustration.

Had the staff responded in this way, it's very possible that Akila would not have escalated to the point of a meltdown. The staff member would have avoided injury, and there would have been no need to involve the police or ambulance. Most importantly, we could have avoided adding new layers of trauma for both Akila and the staff. Moments like these show the power of approaching situations with empathy and a mindset of de-escalation.

This example highlights how reactive, logical responses can escalate a situation, while empathetic, supportive responses can diffuse it. When caregivers and staff approach challenges with curiosity, compassion, and collaboration, the outcomes are often much smoother—not only for the individual with FASD but also for everyone around them.

The Polly Pocket airplane

When we finally started realizing we needed to parent Akila completely differently, I was at a point in life where I hated non-school days. I disliked summer break, spring break, winter break—you name it. These were supposed to be times to relax and enjoy family, but for me, they meant more time for raging and big behaviors. I loved my kids, but the unpredictability of those days often filled me with dread.

One particular day, I was trying to prepare myself for the children arriving home on the bus. I had made a detailed plan for the evening, complete with a written schedule and a list of fun activities. I'd even written everything on a whiteboard and decorated it to look engaging—a rare feat for me since art is not my strong suit. I was determined that this evening would go smoothly.

Akila's bus always arrived home first, and as soon as I saw the way the door swung open, I knew I was in trouble. She burst into the house and immediately declared, "We need to go to the store to buy a Polly Pocket airplane—right now!"

Polly Pockets were her favorite toys at the time—little rubber dolls about three inches tall with a variety of themed accessories. We already had a whole container full of Polly Pocket items: a limousine with a hot tub, jet skis, a camper. But we didn't have an airplane. Apparently, this was a critical oversight.

I tried to redirect her attention to the schedule I had carefully prepared, pointing out the fun activities we could do. She wanted nothing to do with it. I tried to distract her with other Polly Pocket items we already had, but that didn't work either. I suggested we add the airplane to her Christmas list or save up for it. "That's too far away," she said, visibly irritated.

I offered a compromise: "Let's look up the price online and make a chore chart so you can earn it." But no, she needed it now. I even told her we could do the chores today and go get it after Dad came home. "I NEED IT NOW!" she yelled, escalating further.

At this point, my anxiety was climbing through the roof. I knew where this was heading. I desperately wanted to avoid a rage—it felt as if we'd been dealing with non-stop intense outbursts for weeks. Frantically, I tried to come up with another idea.

"Where does Polly want to go on her airplane?" I asked, hoping to spark her imagination. She looked at me as if I'd just asked the dumbest question in the world. But I pressed on. "If Polly needs an airplane, she must be planning a trip. Where does she want to go?"

"Hawaii," Akila said after thinking for a moment.

"Hawaii sounds amazing!" I said. "I've always wanted to go there. Let's fill up the bathtub and pretend it's the ocean. Polly can take her jet skis to Hawaii."

But that wasn't good enough. "Polly's never been on an airplane before," Akila said, "and she wants to fly."

I panicked. I ran madly around the house, searching for anything that resembled an airplane. I thought maybe I could find a toy plane that Polly could fit in. No luck. I found multiple boats and set Polly up in each of them, but Akila was adamant: "No, Polly wants to FLY!"

I tried one last idea. "What if we build an airplane out of LEGOs?" I asked. Akila wasn't having it. She wanted a real Polly

Pocket airplane, and she wanted it *now*. My strategies weren't working, and Akila ended up raging for the entire evening.

Why I share this story

A few years ago, a mentor of mine told me I shouldn't share this story when I train caregivers and professionals. "It didn't work," she said. But that's exactly why I do share it. Caregivers and professionals need to understand that even when you use all the right connected, relational strategies, sometimes it still won't work. It's not because you've failed; it's because the child's brain, in that moment, is not in a place where they can accept the strategies. And that's okay.

When I was training the psychology department at a children's hospital—including neuropsychologists, psychiatrists, and psychologists—I told this story. Afterward, I paused and asked them, "Where did I go wrong? What did I miss?" One doctor raised his hand and said, "Honestly, you thought of way more than I would have." The rest of the room nodded in agreement.

I thanked him and said, "Please remember this when a family comes back to you and says, 'We tried everything, and it didn't work.' Don't tell them to try harder or be more consistent. Instead, tell them:

- 'You're doing a great job.'
- 'You're thinking outside the box, and that matters.'
- 'Put that strategy in your toolbox—it might work next time.'"
- 'We will keep working to add more strategies to your toolbox.'

Key takeaways

1. **Perfection isn't possible:** Nothing will work 100% of the time, no matter how skilled or prepared you are. Accepting this can reduce the guilt and frustration caregivers often feel.

2. **The importance of validation:** Professionals and peers must validate caregivers' efforts and remind them that they are doing their best in an incredibly challenging situation.

3. **Focus on building the toolbox:** Even if a strategy doesn't work in one moment, it might work in another. Keep adding tools to your parenting toolbox.

4. **The power of connection:** While I didn't prevent a rage that evening, my efforts to connect with Akila showed her I was trying. Over time, those moments of connection build trust, even if they don't feel like victories in the moment.

The Polly Pocket airplane story isn't about failure—it's about resilience, creativity, and the reality of parenting a child with FASD. Some days will be hard, and that's okay. What matters is that we keep trying, keep learning, and keep loving. That's how we build hope for our children and ourselves.

BEARS: A brain-based de-escalation strategy

The BEARS strategy (Brain, Emotional age, Anxiety, Relationship, Sensory) is one I developed after a particularly challenging night with Akila. It was her first overnight visit home since the Covid-19 pandemic began in 2020, and we had not been able to see her in person for five months. That night, I discovered her awake in her room with an old cell phone I had carelessly left out in plain sight. For Akila, unsupervised access to electronic devices is incredibly risky and often leads to dangerous situations, even criminal charges.

I entered the dark room and lay down on the floor near her. Speaking softly, I apologized, taking ownership of the situation:

"I'm so sorry for leaving that phone out—that was my mistake. But I really need you to give it back to me." I wish I could say she simply handed it over, but that's not what happened. Instead, she escalated slightly, her voice rising as she told me that she wasn't a child—she was an adult and perfectly capable of handling the phone responsibly.

I stayed calm and remained on the floor, silently brainstorming ways to de-escalate the situation. I tried offering bribes—no success. I tried reasoning with her—still no success. All the while, I watched her use the phone, noting how she was tapping it anxiously, her movements quick and jerky. It was obvious her anxiety was high, and I knew she felt socially connected in that moment, something she often struggles with due to her lack of access to social media. She also started complaining about being hungry, which added another layer to the situation since she hadn't gone to sleep yet.

The breakthrough moment

As I observed her, I began piecing together what was likely happening in her brain. She was probably juggling multiple social media conversations, feeling an urgent need to wrap them up and gather contact information before the device was taken away. This wasn't my first time navigating a situation like this, so I knew I had to find a way to meet her where she was emotionally and mentally.

That's when an idea hit me. I proposed a compromise: "How about this—I'll give you 10 more minutes on the phone while I make scrambled eggs for both of us. Then we'll trade—eggs for the phone." She countered with, "15 minutes," and I agreed. (I've learned to start low so I can allow room for negotiation.)

As I prepared the eggs, I peeked into the room and saw her writing something down and tucking the papers into her backpack. I had a good idea of what she was doing. When the eggs were ready, I brought them to her, and she handed over the phone as promised. We ate together, shared a hug, and finally went to bed. Early the next morning, I checked her backpack and found the paper. She had written down several phone numbers of men she had likely connected with on social media. Knowing the risks, I altered a few of the numbers slightly—turning ones into sevens, for example—before putting the paper back. Let's just say I've made peace with the occasional white lie or sneaky digit swap—if creative math keeps her safe, I'll take my chances with karma.

The birth of BEARS

This experience got me thinking more deeply about what was happening in her brain during moments of dysregulation. It also pushed me to develop a more systematic way of understanding and responding to her behaviors in a connected and compassionate manner. That's how I came up with BEARS—a simple yet powerful tool for de-escalating challenging situations.

BEARS: The framework

1. **Brain first:** Pause and consider what is happening in their brain. Are they operating from their logical, thinking brain, or has their survival brain (fight/flight/freeze) taken over? Approach the situation with this awareness in mind.

2. **Emotional age:** Quickly assess their emotional age in the moment. Remember, this can shift depending on the situation and stress levels. If they're acting more like a frustrated five-year-old than their chronological age, meet them where they are emotionally.

3. **Anxiety origin:** Reflect on what might be triggering their anxiety. What's driving their behavior? Is it sensory overload, fear of losing connection, or perhaps hunger or exhaustion? Identifying the origin of their anxiety helps guide your response.

4. **Relational connection:** Ask yourself: Can my response strengthen our connection? Whether it's through validating their feelings, offering physical comfort, or just being present, prioritize the relationship.

5. **Sensory intervention:** Think about what sensory strategies might help regulate them. Would a snack, deep pressure (like a hug), a cool drink, or a calming activity like listening to music help them return to a regulated state?

Why BEARS works

BEARS emphasizes understanding and meeting the individual's needs in the moment. It moves away from traditional, punitive approaches and instead focuses on empathy, connection, and brain-based responses. By considering their developmental profile, emotional state, and sensory needs, BEARS allows caregivers to intervene in ways that are more likely to de-escalate the situation and build trust.

This framework has transformed the way I approach challenging moments with Akila and has provided a structure I can share with other caregivers and professionals. It's not a one-size-fits-all solution, but it's a starting point for understanding and responding with compassion in difficult situations.

Chapter 7

The Storm Within: Understanding and Managing Rages

Raging

Most of you have witnessed a toddler tantrum—they're exhausting and emotionally draining, and they always seem to last forever. Now imagine that same tantrum in a 10-year-old or a 15-year-old. They're in a much larger body, likely raging with hormones, and still struggling to control their emotions. Whether we call it raging, aggression, meltdowns, or dysregulation, one thing is certain: it's not fun. It's not fun for the caregiver or adult trying to help, and it's even less fun for the child or adolescent experiencing the meltdown.

As mentioned earlier, aggression often stems from several impaired brain domains, but it's most closely tied to a lack of impulse control. Recently, an amazing self-advocate living with fetal alcohol spectrum disorder (FASD) taught me something that completely changed how I think about these moments. Rebecca Tillou, author of *Tenacity*, shared that many individuals with FASD exhibit aggression as a way to make their anger or frustration tangible. It becomes a concrete way for them to experience and express what they are feeling internally.

Think about how we often make our positive emotions tangible—when we're happy, we might hug or kiss someone. For individuals with FASD, aggression can serve as a way to make overwhelming emotions, like frustration or anger, feel more real and manageable. This insight was a eureka moment for me. I've been training on raging for years, but I had never considered it from this perspective. Thank you, Rebecca, for teaching me this invaluable lesson—you are truly amazing.

Akila's raging started as a toddler, and it became more intense with each passing year. My husband and I were desperate for help, seeking advice from doctors, therapists, books, seminars—anywhere we could find ideas to eliminate or at least decrease the raging. But nothing worked.

The aggression began to take a toll on our family. The stress created a toxic environment in our home, and I started experiencing between three and five migraines a week. These weren't just minor headaches—I'd be shut in a dark room, vomiting, unable to function. The aggression wasn't just affecting me; it was beginning to negatively impact our other children in profound ways.

We turned to our social services for support, hoping to find interventions and strategies that could help us survive this storm. One suggestion was in-home therapy.

When the Professionals Witness What We Live Every Day

We were hopeful when the county suggested in-home therapy—it seemed like a solution that might bring much-needed relief and guidance. The idea of having a professional come into our home to observe and provide hands-on support was appealing. It meant they could see the full scope of what we were dealing with and tailor strategies to our specific situation.

Our first experience with in-home therapy started off with promise. The therapist, Joan, was kind, patient, and genuinely interested in understanding Akila. She observed the dynamics in our home, talked with our other children, and took the time to listen to our frustrations. She came equipped with tools and suggestions, but they didn't seem to fit the unique challenges of Akila's brain. Joan was about my age at the time and new in her role; she was still under supervision and needed more hours before she would be fully licensed.

During our intake meeting with Joan, my husband and I shared Akila's history and the struggles we were facing. At the end of the meeting, Joan said something that won us both over: "I can tell you both know a lot about FASD, much more than I do. I'm willing to work with Akila, and I would really like to help her, but I will need a lot of guidance and support from both of you."

I cannot express how refreshing it was to hear this level of honesty. She wasn't pretending to have all the answers or making promises she couldn't keep. She acknowledged our expertise as parents and collaborators. It was such a relief not to have someone come in, blowing smoke up our you-know-whats.

One of the initial approaches Joan shared involved structured behavior plans—clear rules and expectations with rewards and consequences for compliance or non-compliance. It sounded good in theory, but it quickly became clear that these plans were ineffective. Akila's impulsivity and inability to connect actions with long-term outcomes rendered these strategies useless. The therapist kept tweaking the plans, but the raging continued, and our hope began to dwindle.

Joan worked with us for a little over a year before moving on to a different position. She wasn't perfect—no one is—but she genuinely tried to connect with Akila and adapt her approach as she learned more. One week, during one of her sessions, something happened that highlighted both the challenges and small victories of our journey.

Michael wasn't home from work yet, and I was in the kitchen doing dishes. The other kids were in the back of the house, and Joan and Akila were in the living room talking. The week before, Joan had taken Akila to the library, and Akila was now pushing for Joan to take her again. Joan explained that she had other plans for their session, but Akila wasn't having it.

I could feel my anxiety rising as I anticipated what was likely to happen next—meaning I knew she would come to complain to me shortly. Within minutes, Akila stormed into the kitchen, visibly upset. She started complaining to me that Joan wouldn't take her to the library. I tried to redirect her. "Oh, it would be fun to go to the library! It's been a few weeks since we've gone. How about we go after school tomorrow?"

That didn't work. Akila began escalating, calling names and getting louder. Joan came into the kitchen and tried to help, enthusiastically suggesting, "Akila, let's go play Uno!"

Akila spun around and snapped, "Shut the f**k up, you bleach-blonde b***h!" For the record, Joan had red hair. Joan wisely stayed silent. Many adults would have kept talking, trying to reason with her, but Joan had good instincts.

Akila turned back to me, and I kept trying to distract her. "What is it that you want to get from the library? A book? A movie? A CD?" She wasn't calming down.

I glanced at a poster on the kitchen wall that Joan and Akila had made together months earlier. It was covered with sticky notes listing calming strategies they had brainstormed. "I'm starting to feel anxious and stressed," I said. "I'm going to pick a calming strategy from the poster. Would you like to choose one too?"

Her answer was no, accompanied by a string of expletives. Before I could say another word, she lunged at me, swinging her fist to punch me in the face. I managed to grab her wrists mid-swing, holding them firmly. This was usually the point where she would start to kick or headbutt.

Just then, Michael walked in the front door, arriving home from work.

Years of dealing with verbal and physical aggression had taught us that distraction can sometimes work to de-escalate Akila. It doesn't always succeed, but when it does, it's like catching a lifeline. That evening, Michael noticed animal tracks in the snow as he walked up to the house. Thinking quickly, he used it as a distraction.

With great enthusiasm, he called out, "Akila, come here! I need your help tracking an animal in the yard!"

Akila immediately dropped everything, grabbed her coat and boots, and ran outside with him to investigate.

Joan and I sat down at the dining room table, both of us still catching our breath. Joan, looking stunned, said, "What the f**k? Is this what happens every day?"

"Pretty much," I replied.

"What did I do wrong? What should I have done differently?" She shook her head.

"Honestly, you did everything I—and most professionals—would recommend. You did a really good job."

I asked her to document what had just happened and share it with the rest of Akila's care team. It always felt as if no one believed us when we said we were implementing their strategies, yet the rages persisted. This was a pivotal moment. Joan's validation and documentation helped us secure the proper supports for Akila, finally moving us toward a system that understood her needs.

The role of Michael and the importance of teamwork

Michael's role in this story highlights something crucial: the importance of teamwork in parenting a child with FASD. He didn't come home expecting to walk into chaos (well, he probably was expecting it, to be honest), but he stayed calm and thought on his feet. His ability to assess the situation, remember the animal tracks, and use them as a distraction made all the difference that evening. For those of you who are single caregivers, I see you, and I acknowledge how much more challenging it must be to handle situations like this on your own.

It's moments like these that underscore how critical it is for caregivers to work together, to have each other's backs, and to recognize each other's strengths. Michael often serves as a grounding force in our family, able to swoop in with fresh energy when I've reached my limit. This isn't to say everything always works perfectly—far from it—but when we approach challenges as a team, the outcomes are often better for everyone, especially Akila.

The long-term impact

This incident was pivotal not just in helping us get the right supports for Akila but also in validating our struggles as parents. Too often, caregivers are dismissed or blamed for their child's behaviors, which can be incredibly isolating and demoralizing. Joan's acknowledgment that we were doing everything "right" was a turning point for me.

It also reinforced an important lesson—even when strategies don't "work" in the moment, the effort is not wasted. Every time we try to use distraction, offer a calming strategy, or engage Akila in a positive way, we are reinforcing pathways in her brain that help her regulate emotions in the long run.

Michael's quick thinking, Joan's support, and our persistence as a family helped us navigate that night—and many nights after. It's not about always getting it right but about showing up, staying present, and trying again.

Triggers and zones of regulation

As I mentioned earlier, we were desperate and seeking help from everyone we could. Whenever I attended a conference, I would wait for the professional to finish their session, and my hand would shoot up during the Q&A. My question was always the same: "Thanks for all of that information, but what do we do about the raging?"

Too often, the response was to suggest some version of a sticker chart. To me, this was an immediate signal that the professional did not truly understand FASD.

Another common piece of advice was to chart behaviors and look for patterns or triggers that might be avoided. We tried this for quite a while and were actually able to make some changes. By identifying patterns, we learned that some of Akila's rages were tied to sensory issues or other concrete factors, allowing us to make adjustments and avoid some of the outbursts.

However, one trigger remained unavoidable: not getting what she wanted immediately when she wanted it. No matter how much we strategized, this was a challenge we couldn't eliminate. So the rages continued.

Another frequent recommendation from professionals was to use distraction, and this became one of our most effective tools. Michael, in particular, is the most gifted distractor I've ever encountered. He has an incredible ability to "unstick" Akila when she's fixated, and watching him work encouraged me to think more creatively about distractions.

One time, when Akila was about 20 years old, I was driving her and her boyfriend, Mowgli, back to their group homes after a date. As we were driving, Akila began escalating into a verbal rage. Verbal aggression is often one step away from physical aggression, which is never fun—especially in the confined space of a moving car.

There are the zones of regulation: the *green zone*, where everyone is calm, happy, and in a good mood; the *yellow zone*, where stress and anxiety start to increase; and the *red zone*, which represents full-blown rage and extreme dysregulation. As Akila's behavior escalated in the backseat, I realized she was already deep in the yellow zone and teetering on the edge of the red zone. I knew that if I drove her straight to her group home in this state, the dysregulation would intensify and likely result in a full-blown meltdown by the time we arrived.

Instead, I chose a different approach. I began driving aimlessly around quiet residential neighborhoods, maintaining a calm demeanor and trying to wait her out. My goal was to give her space and time to self-regulate, or at least to prevent her escalation from worsening.

Forty-five minutes later, she was still in a verbal rage—yelling, cursing, threatening, and being belligerent. Mowgli was sitting quietly, clearly trying not to add fuel to the fire. My patience was wearing thin, and I knew I needed a new approach. I had already tried several distraction tactics, all of which failed.

Then, I came up with an idea.

It was a warm August evening in Minnesota, still light outside but with the sun starting to set. I stopped the car in the middle of a quiet residential street—not pulling to the side, just stopping. I rolled down all the windows, cranked up their playlist, and stepped out of the car.

And then I started dancing.

For the record, I am not a good dancer. In fact, I was deliberately trying to dance even less well than my natural lack of rhythm would allow. My goal wasn't to impress anyone but to get them laughing. At first, Akila didn't even notice. She was lying down in the back seat, still yelling and completely absorbed in her frustration. But then Mowgli leaned over to her and said, "Look at Mama!"

And that was the turning point. She sat up, glanced out the window, and froze for a moment before bursting into laughter. That laughter was exactly what I had hoped for—it was the crack in the storm that let some light through. Mowgli joined in, laughing and pointing, and suddenly the mood shifted. I opened their car door, grabbed their hands, and pulled them out to dance with me.

We danced in the middle of that residential street for at least 20 minutes—maybe even 30. Curious neighbors peeked out of their windows, but no one called the police (which has happened to us before, though not because of my dancing). We FaceTimed a couple of friends and even recorded a video to upload to Instagram. (I later deleted the video—a decision I now regret, as it would have been a great teaching tool in my trainings.)

The dancing wasn't just about getting them to laugh. I knew that if I'd stopped at just making them laugh, Akila likely would have re-escalated on the drive home. But by involving her in the dancing, I turned it into a regulatory activity. The physical movement and sensory input helped calm her brain and body. I was able to drop them off at their homes without further challenges.

Years ago, I wouldn't have handled it this way. I would have lost my patience, said things that pushed her further into the red zone, and unintentionally escalated the situation. I now realize how much we, as parents, had contributed to her rages in the past—and that's a tough pill to swallow.

The art of distraction

It's important to note that distractions won't work every time. Some professionals might suggest otherwise, but I disagree. There will be days when even your most creative distraction will fail. This simply means that, in that moment, your child's brain is buffering too much to engage. When this happens, it's okay to move on.

That said, distractions remain one of the most valuable tools in your arsenal. Over the years, I've learned to think outside the box when trying to distract Akila. Here are a few ideas to get you into the right mindset for creating effective distractions.

Car rages: Strategies for safety and connection

Car rages are never fun and can be quite dangerous. When a situation escalates to the point where safety is a concern, I recommend pulling over as soon as possible. One time, Akila and I were stuck in traffic, and I could feel her starting to escalate. My own post-traumatic stress disorder (PTSD) often kicks in during these moments, making it hard to think of effective distractions or meet her in a connected, relational way. This is why it's crucial for caregivers to do the work of keeping their own systems as regulated as possible, especially when their child is dysregulated.

That day, I managed to keep my brain from overloading and came up with an idea. I rolled down my window and yelled at the top of my lungs, "MOVE OUT OF THE WAY, PEOPLE! AKILA IS IN A HURRY!" She looked at me like I had lost my mind and irritably asked what I was doing. I told her that since she seemed to be in a hurry, I was trying to clear the traffic for her. Then, I pushed the button to roll down her window and invited her to join me. To my relief, we both ended up yelling and laughing hysterically.

This spontaneous distraction not only diffused the situation but became a tradition. Now, whenever we're stuck in traffic, we start yelling silly things out of the windows and laughing. It's a quirky but effective way for us to connect.

Distraction: The fake phone call

Another distraction I've used when Akila enters the yellow zone is pretending to receive a dramatic phone call. For example, I'll answer my phone and exclaim, "Hello? Oh no! What hospital are you at?" Immediately, Akila's curiosity is piqued, and she wants to know what's happening. I tell her to hold on while I "ask" a few more questions and then hang up on the fake caller. I explain, "One of my families has a child who is raging and ended up in the emergency room. They need help. You've been there for raging—what advice should I give them?"

She gets really excited and wants to help. I then say, "Hold on, I need to grab some paper and a pen so we can write this down." I step into the next room and intentionally take my time, dilly-dallying for a few minutes. This gives her some space to self-regulate. However, I'm careful not to leave her waiting too long, as that could backfire.

When I return, I hand her the pen and paper and ask her to do the writing herself. Writing serves as a sensory activity that helps regulate her brain. She eagerly comes up with ideas, and I usually add a few suggestions to keep the momentum going. Once the list is complete, I make my pretend call back to the imaginary person, enthusiastically sharing her advice.

After "hanging up," I high-five her and say, "Let's go and get a treat—you just helped someone!" Crisis averted. Not only is the situation diffused, but her involvement and sense of accomplishment also help restore a positive connection.

I realize this approach may not be considered "honest" by some and might even be labeled as lying. In my world, I'm entirely comfortable with these "white lies" if they help prevent a rage. After the trauma the entire family has endured over the years with raging and the PTSD caused by it, it's easy to make concessions in this area.

Every family has to find what works for them. If this approach doesn't sit well with you, that's okay—there's no judgment here. You need to choose strategies that align with your values and provide the best outcomes for your child and family.

The importance of documenting and recycling strategies

Distractions like these are not foolproof or repeatable every time. If I were to use the fake phone call tactic too often, she'd catch on. This is why I encourage families and caregivers to document these situations, including:

- Date and time.
- What and when they last ate or drank.
- What triggered the escalation.
- What distractions were tried and whether they worked.
- What could be done differently next time.
- Any identifiable patterns or causes of anxiety.

Documenting helps identify patterns that might allow you to avoid certain triggers altogether. Equally important, it helps you remember and recycle effective distractions. You'd be surprised how easy it is to forget even the most brilliant strategies! By keeping track, you'll know when it's safe to try a previously successful distraction again after enough time has passed.

Keeping calm as a caregiver

Another piece of advice we received from professionals was to keep ourselves calm. While this sounds simple, it's incredibly challenging in the heat of the moment. Oddly enough, both my husband and I are naturally calm people—we're not yellers by nature. Even so, we had to work hard to extend the amount of time we could remain patient during a rage. On most days, I can stay calm for about two hours, which I've learned is far longer than many people can manage. Most caregivers I work with are lucky to last 10–15 minutes before their patience runs out.

The last resort: Calling emergency services

It is important to recognize that caregivers may sometimes need to call emergency services for safety reasons. However, this option comes with significant challenges. It can add a new layer of trauma for everyone involved, and there is always a risk that the situation could escalate, potentially resulting in harm to the child.

Taking a child to the hospital emergency department is another commonly suggested option by professionals. While this might be necessary to ensure the safety of the child and family, it also presents its own challenges. It can be very expensive in the U.S., depending on insurance coverage, and it is typically a short-term solution. If a child is admitted as an inpatient, the stay is usually brief and focused solely on stabilization.

In many areas, mobile crisis units are available and can sometimes provide helpful support. However, their effectiveness depends on several factors, such as how quickly they can respond, and whether the staff are properly trained in what to say and, just as importantly, what not to say. Unfortunately, both my personal experience and stories from families I've worked with have revealed instances where crisis workers made inappropriate or counterproductive comments to children during these critical moments.

Professionals also advised us to call 911 (emergency services in the U.S.) if we didn't feel safe. While this is sound advice, it often left us feeling isolated and alone. The reality was that, although we managed to slightly reduce the frequency of Akila's rages with distractions and other strategies, she was still raging almost daily—often multiple times a day.

We were living in a nightmare, one that was not only emotionally exhausting but also deeply scary. Despite the well-meaning advice we received, we still felt trapped in a cycle of chaos, desperate for something more to help our family heal.

Handling rages from children or adolescents with FASD is incredibly challenging, and one of the hardest things to accept is how much we, as caregivers, might unintentionally escalate the situation. Over time, I've learned—often the hard way—what doesn't work, what makes things worse, and what I need to avoid.

The turning point: Lessons from Jordan

When Akila was a teenager, we began providing respite care for teenage boys with FASD. There is such a need for respite for families like ours and we decided it was time to give back. We had figured out a lot of strategies to support Akila's FASD, and wanted to help families I worked with. One of those teens, Jordan, had stayed with us many times. One particular week, I took Jordan, Akila, and two of my other kids to a movie. On the way home, Akila started to rage in the car. It was one of the big ones. I had to pull over into an empty parking lot to try to manage the situation.

We were in that parking lot for nearly an hour, and it was an incredibly stressful experience. Akila was chasing us around with an ice scraper, throwing things, kicking, and hitting. My goal is always to avoid calling the police unless I feel like we're truly in danger. I'm not saying you shouldn't call the police if you feel unsafe—every situation is different. But for us, calling the police is a decision that carries additional weight.

My husband and I are both white, and our children are Black. This adds an extra dynamic that we must carefully consider when involving law enforcement. While I deeply respect law enforcement as a profession—my youngest son, Zeke, is completing his final year at university to pursue a career in law enforcement—I also acknowledge the reality. People of color are statistically more likely to be harmed during encounters with the police, especially during mental health crises. Ignoring this truth is to live in denial of a significant societal issue.

This is not an indictment of individual police officers, many of whom are doing their best in challenging situations. But as a parent, I must weigh every risk and prioritize the safety of my children. That day in the parking lot, we managed to get through the crisis without further escalation, but it was a stark reminder of how complex these situations can be.

On this evening, with patience, I was able to wait Akila out and she finally regulated. Afterward, I got all of the kids in bed and I stayed up late with Jordan to process the event. He surprised me by offering invaluable insights.

He pointed out how much it bothered him that I kept telling Akila to "calm down." He explained it felt condescending and frustrating when people had said the same thing to him during his rages. He also told me how annoying it was when I repeated her name over and over, and that my slow, deliberate tone came across as patronizing. Then, in a raw and honest moment, he said, "You talk to her like she's retarded."

At first, this stung. I thought I was being calm and helpful, but his feedback made me realize that what I thought was regulating behavior might actually come off as dismissive or disrespectful, especially for older children and teens. His perspective shifted how I approached dysregulation, and it's shaped how I train others today.

Things not to do during a rage

Through years of trial, error, and learning from individuals with FASD, I've developed a list of things to avoid when dealing with dysregulated behavior. That said, every child is different, and caregivers must trust their instincts about what works best.

1. **Don't tell them to calm down:** This phrase is often perceived as dismissive and can escalate the situation further. I found a quote on the internet which hits this point home: "Never in the history of calming down, has anyone ever calmed down by being told to calm down!"

2. **Don't repeat their name:** Unless you're trying to get their attention, avoid saying their name repeatedly. It can feel like nagging or condescension.

3. **Don't speak slowly (for older children):** While a slower tone might help small children, older kids may perceive it as patronizing. Use a natural, calm voice instead.

4. **Avoid terms of endearment:** Some kids find "sweetie" or "honey" comforting, but others may find it patronizing or irritating. Know what works for your child; this is age dependent also.

5. **Don't point out consequences:** Mentioning consequences during a rage can feel like a threat. This triggers their fight-or-flight response, pushing them deeper into the red zone.

6. **Don't respond to cursing or threats:** Addressing inappropriate language or threats in the moment won't be effective. Save the discussion for when they are regulated.

7. **Don't minimize their feelings:** Avoid saying things like "It's no big deal" or "This is easy to fix." What may seem minor to you feels monumental to them. Dismissing their feelings invalidates their experience.

8. **Be mindful of eye contact:** Neither dismissive nor intimidating eye contact is helpful. Strike a balance by being present without staring them down.

9. **Don't use logic:** When they're dysregulated, their brain is in fight-or-flight mode and logic won't land. Save reasoning for when they're calm, and even then, logic may not be effective.

10. **Stop talking:** The more we talk, the harder it is for their overwhelmed brain to process. Silence can be one of the most powerful tools.

I know this is a long list of what not to do—but don't worry, the list of what to do is much shorter (and I'll be sharing those tips shortly). The key takeaway is this: during a rage, it's often us—the well-meaning adults—who unintentionally make things worse by reacting in ways that feel natural but aren't effective for a dysregulated brain. The good news? With a few small shifts, we can make a big difference.

Understanding the brain during dysregulation

When a child with FASD is in the yellow or red zone, they are operating from their amygdala—the part of the brain responsible for fight, flight, freeze, or fawn responses. In this state, they are unable to process language, reason, or consequences. Talking or reprimanding them in this state often backfires.

As I began reflecting more on what happens in the brain and body during moments of stress or conflict, I couldn't help but think about arguments between Michael and me. If he tells me to "calm down" when I'm upset about something, it doesn't go well—it actually pushes me further into the red zone. And if he says my name while we're arguing, that would absolutely trigger me even more.

It made me realize how I used to respond to Akila when she entered the yellow or red zone, and how ineffective—and even counterproductive—my approach was. I'd often go into repeat mode, thinking I was helping. A typical response might have sounded like this: "Akila, it's okay. This is no big deal. Calm down. Honey, calm down. You don't need to get so upset. Please, Akila, we can fix this. Akiiiiillla, caaaalm dooowwwnnn. Akila, honey, calm down."

Looking back, I can see how the constant repetition, the tone, and even the words themselves likely came across as condescending or dismissive, escalating her emotions instead of calming her down. At the time, I thought I was modeling calmness, but now I understand that what she really needed was space, validation, and strategies to help her regulate—not an endless loop of "calm down" commands. It was a lesson I had to learn the hard way, but one that changed how I approach her dysregulation entirely.

Learning to stay silent

One of the hardest lessons I had to learn was the importance of silence. When Akila would verbally rage, my instinct was to argue or correct her perceptions, especially when they were wildly inaccurate. Over time, I realized this only escalated her further. Eventually, I trained myself to stay quiet during these moments, and it made a significant difference.

Validating their experience

Even when the rage is about something seemingly small or illogical—like running out of their favorite cereal—it's important to validate their feelings. To them, it's not a small issue; it's a mountain. Saying, "I understand this is really upsetting for you," rather than dismissing their emotions, can de-escalate the situation.

For some kids, asking a supportive question in moments of dysregulation—such as, "What do you need from me right now?" or, "How can I help you?"—may be effective. It shows that you are listening and care about their needs. However, for many children with FASD, their brain is too overwhelmed to process or respond to a question during these moments. For example, I cannot ask Akila a question when she is dysregulated—it only escalates her further.

Instead, I use simple, supportive statements at intervals that feel appropriate, maybe every five to eight minutes. Phrases like, "I'm sorry you're feeling this way" or, "I'm here for you, and I'll stay as long as you need," can provide a sense of safety and support.

It's important to recognize that these statements might not be received as intended in the moment. Akila might respond with threats or accusations, like shouting, "YOU DON'T CARE ABOUT ME!" To me, this is a signal that she's still deep in the red zone, and it's not yet time to try to resolve or de-escalate further. Once a child is fully dysregulated, the focus needs to shift to waiting it out with patience and calm.

Sometimes, Akila gets upset if I'm not talking enough, especially if she's asking repetitive questions in an attempt to get an answer she likes. Continuing to answer her at this stage only keeps her brain in overdrive, cycling through processing and reprocessing without resolution. In these moments, I don't engage. If she gets upset with my silence, I might say something like, "I'm feeling stressed right now and trying to keep myself calm." This is true, and it models self-regulation. After all, my own calm is the only thing I can fully control in these intense moments.

Trauma fog

Both the child and the caregiver can experience what is known as "trauma fog" after a rage or stressful event. During this fog, concentration, processing, and decision-making can be impaired. Trying to have "the talk" while still in this state often leads to frustration for both parties. Waiting until the child is in a "good brain place" is crucial for meaningful communication.

The "talk"

Having "the talk" with a child or adolescent after a rage is a delicate process that requires mindfulness about timing, purpose, and the state of the child's brain. For neurotypical individuals without significant trauma, it can take nearly two hours for their bodies to return to baseline after a stressful event. For neurodivergent individuals with trauma histories, this recovery period can extend to 24 hours or longer.

Yet caregivers often sit down with a child 15 minutes or an hour after a rage, attempting to address what happened. For most of these young people, this timing isn't effective. They are still far from a calm and regulated state, making it difficult for them to process or benefit from the conversation. That said, there are exceptions: some children may need to discuss the event right away to avoid perseverating on what upset them. For these outliers, immediate processing might prevent re-escalation.

What will "the talk" accomplish?

It's worth questioning whether "the talk" is necessary after every rage or behavior. The intent of these discussions is often to teach the child skills to handle emotions differently in the future. However, for individuals with FASD, these conversations may even harm their self-esteem and the caregiver–child relationship.

While it's important to address certain behaviors, being selective about when to have these discussions is key. For example, if rages occur frequently, it's not practical—or beneficial—to address every single incident. Instead, choose moments that are strategic and meaningful.

A-ha moment for group home staff

During training for my daughter Akila's group home staff, one of the staff members shared an incident where Akila had been very rude and demanding about getting cereal and yogurt, which she typically gets herself every morning. The staff member engaged in a power struggle with her over her tone, which escalated into a larger issue. He asked if he should have handled the situation differently.

I asked how Akila's manners typically were when she wasn't upset. All the staff agreed that she was usually polite and had excellent manners. I explained that when she is rude and demanding, it's a cue that her brain is dysregulated. While it's difficult to endure disrespectful behavior, I recommended that he simply respond by saying he'd be happy to get her cereal and yogurt for her.

The staff member then asked if he should later talk to her about being more respectful once she was calm. I posed the question: What would the goal of that conversation be? Akila already knows how to use manners when her brain is regulated. However, when her brain is "on fire," she lacks the capacity to access those learned behaviors. Trying to teach her in that moment is unlikely to be effective and may only harm their relationship and her self-esteem.

Guidelines for "the talk"

We need to be strategic about when and how to approach these conversations. Here are some guidelines:

- **Preferred person:** Choose someone the child has a strong relationship with to lead the discussion when possible.

- **Right moment:** Wait until the child is in a calm, regulated state.

- **Keep it brief:** Long lectures or drawn-out discussions can be overwhelming. A short, focused conversation is more effective.

- **Clear purpose:** Be clear on the goal of the talk. Are you addressing a specific issue or trying to build a skill? Avoid unnecessary conversations that may not lead to meaningful outcomes. Be very careful not to shame them for how they acted.

By being thoughtful about how and when we approach "the talk," we can foster better relationships and focus on what truly helps the child grow.

A work in progress

No caregiver is perfect, and learning how to navigate rages takes time, patience, and self-compassion. While we can't control every rage, we *can* adjust our own responses to create an environment where our kids feel more understood and supported. These strategies may not eliminate the challenges entirely, but they can reduce their intensity and frequency over time.

With Akila, we learned, unfortunately far too late, that some of the things we thought were helpful—and even strategies recommended by professionals—were actually escalating Akila's rages. Our actions and words often caused her to rage more frequently, go higher into the red zone, and stay there longer. Realizing this was heartbreaking. As parents, you want to help your child, not worsen their struggles.

This painful realization is one of the reasons I am so passionate about training others. I want to spare you the trial-and-error process we endured and help you avoid the mistakes we made. The journey is ongoing, and while there's no perfect path, together we can work toward more effective and compassionate ways to support our kids through their hardest moments.

Chapter 8

Why They Lie: Understanding the Reasons

The challenge of lying and confabulation

Nobody likes being lied to. It erodes trust, damages relationships, and can lead to frustration and misunderstanding. However, many individuals with fetal alcohol spectrum disorder (FASD) struggle with something that looks like lying but isn't. Instead, it's a phenomenon called *confabulation*.

Confabulation is when a person's brain unintentionally fills in memory gaps with inaccurate or false information. The person isn't deliberately trying to deceive; their brain creates these "memories" to make sense of missing or incomplete information. Confabulation can be so intense that it generates entirely false memories, which the person genuinely believes to be true.

How confabulation differs from lying

Lying is intentional and often done with a purpose—whether to avoid consequences, gain an advantage, or protect oneself.

Confabulation, on the other hand, is entirely unintentional. The person isn't trying to manipulate; they truly believe the inaccurate information they're presenting.

While confabulation can happen to anyone, it's particularly common in small children, whose brains haven't fully matured, and in individuals with FASD, traumatic brain injury, and dementia. As neurotypical children grow, their brains develop, and confabulation naturally decreases. For individuals with FASD, however, confabulation can persist into adolescence and adulthood.

Caregivers often make the assumption that the confabulation is intentional and being done to avoid something, but it rarely is, even when it seems like it. People will often ask me how they figure out if the child is lying or confabulating. My answer is that it doesn't matter. Approach it the same way without shaming the child, using the strategy outlined below in this chapter.

Everyday examples of confabulation

Even neurotypical brains confabulate. Have you ever had an argument with a friend or partner that goes something like this:

- You: "I told you about this."
- Them: "No, you didn't."
- You: "Yes, I did."
- Them: "No, you absolutely didn't."

You both remember the situation differently, and neither of you is lying. One of your brains has filled in the gaps incorrectly.

I remember one time vividly: I planned a trip to Sioux Falls with some high school friends. After our call, I thought about how I'd tell my husband, Michael, and even rehearsed the conversation in my head. The week of the trip, I asked him which car I should take, and he said, "What trip? You didn't tell me about this." I argued that I had—but eventually, I realized that I'd never actually told him; I'd only thought about telling him. My brain was convinced I had because I had rehearsed it so clearly. Classic confabulation.

Confabulation in individuals with FASD

For individuals with FASD, confabulation often occurs on a more frequent and dramatic scale. For example, they might insist they turned in their homework, even while you're holding it ungraded in your hand; or they may claim they cleaned their room, even though it's obviously still messy. In these cases, they're not lying but recalling other instances when they *did* turn in homework or cleaned their room. Their brain substitutes old memories for the present situation.

Sometimes, confabulation goes even further, creating elaborate and highly unrealistic stories. For example, they might describe something like, "I met a movie star on the way to school today," when no such thing happened; or they may recount entire events that never took place, such as winning a contest or traveling somewhere they've never been. These stories often sound like deliberate lies, but they're not. The person's brain is doing its best to "fill in the blanks."

Confabulation isn't unique to FASD. It's also common in individuals with various forms of dementia. For example, my friend Julie's sister, who has dementia, once told Julie that I had texted her about winning the Publishers Clearinghouse sweepstakes. None of this was true—I didn't win, I didn't even enter to win, and I certainly didn't send that text—but Julie's sister wasn't lying. Her brain had created this memory.

When someone with FASD (or another condition) confabulates, it's crucial to approach the situation with empathy and understanding. Calling them a liar or accusing them of dishonesty won't help—it can damage trust and hurt their self-esteem. Ultimately, confabulation is a symptom of the brain injury that FASD represents—not a reflection of the person's character.

The reality of confabulation: A life lesson

One of Akila's most infamous confabulations happened when she had stolen yet another cell phone. Over the years, she had taken countless phones. This was during the time when we were still using consequences and punishments, rather than connected relational parenting. When I confronted her with the phone, she confabulated an elaborate story: she told me the phone belonged to Justin Bieber. Apparently, Justin had been at her school that day and had *given* her his phone (he was not at her school).

Realistic, right? Absolutely not. But in my old way of thinking, I felt the need to "catch her" in the lie. Back then, I believed it was essential for her to admit to the lie so I could punish her and teach her a lesson about trustworthiness. Looking back, I shudder at the strategies we used. The more I pushed her, the more fantastical her story became.

Akila elaborated that Justin had performed at a school assembly that morning, changed outfits four times, and sang more than 40 songs. Not only that, but Selena Gomez had been there with him. The more I interrogated her, the more details she invented. Determined to prove her wrong, I looked up Justin Bieber's tour schedule on my computer. He was performing that evening in Brazil. Feeling triumphant, I thought I had finally "won" this power struggle.

But Akila doubled down. She calmly explained that his

performance happened during the first hour of school, leaving him plenty of time to fly to Brazil for his evening concert.

And you know what? She was technically right! He *could* have made it in time. How did she even figure that out? Akila can't remember what 2 × 2 equals or recall the name of a new friend she's just met, but somehow she managed to calculate that Justin Bieber's jet-setting timeline was plausible.

A shift in perspective

A few days later, when Akila's brain was more regulated, I brought up the phone incident again. Unsurprisingly, she brushed it off, claiming that I had misunderstood her earlier. Over time, I stopped revisiting these incidents.

What I eventually realized is that most of Akila's confabulations—and likely many of the "lies" told by individuals with FASD—aren't intentional. They often occur when anxiety is high, and the brain isn't functioning properly. These confabulations are the brain's attempt to fill in gaps or create coherence in moments of stress or uncertainty. They are often an attempt to fit in somewhere as well.

High-anxiety moments that trigger confabulation

Confabulation is most likely to occur when anxiety spikes. Here are four common triggers:

1. When they are in trouble or think they're in trouble.
2. When they are trying to socially fit in.
3. When they are trying to recall something they think they should remember.
4. When they are trying to understand something they think they should comprehend.

Teaching Akila about confabulation

Several years ago, we started teaching Akila about the concept of confabulation. Here's what we say: "Because of your brain injury, your brain sometimes tries to confuse you or trick you into thinking something is true that isn't. You have to let us—your parents, staff at your group home, or school—help you know when your brain is confabulating. Otherwise, people might think you're lying, and they won't want to be around you."

This strategy has worked remarkably well.

Now, when Akila starts to confabulate and I gently remind her of this explanation, she often lets out a frustrated "ugh" and quickly changes the subject. Even better, there have been times when she has caught herself mid-confabulation, asking, "Mom, is my brain doing that big word?" (She often forgets the term "confabulation.")

The first time this happened, we celebrated by taking her out to dinner. It was a huge win.

A word on false allegations

If you have a child who confabulates, there is a risk of facing false allegations. Unfortunately, when a child's anxiety spikes, their brain may fill in the gaps with dramatic stories, which can sometimes include false allegations of abuse. This is not intentional, even though it may feel that way in the moment.

First, stay calm and don't blame the child. It's critical not to get upset with the child. False allegations are not a deliberate attempt to harm you, but rather a reflection of how their brain processes anxiety and stress. In our experience, when our daughter made false allegations, it almost always occurred with new people in situations where her anxiety was heightened and she didn't know what to say. Her brain filled in the gaps with misinformation.

Second, don't blame the system. While it may be frustrating, don't get angry with the system for investigating. Child Protective Services (CPS) in the U.S. and mandated reporting exist to protect children, and this process is essential. If you know your child is prone to confabulations, it's important to document these incidents thoroughly. Keeping a record can protect your family, provide clarity to professionals, and ultimately help your child.

The importance of communication and documentation

When Akila was in third grade, I informed her Individualized Education Program (IEP) team that she frequently lied and that dramatic stories she shared were likely not true. I assured them I would notify them of any legitimate issues within our family. My decision came after an incident where her principal called me, concerned because Akila told her I had stomach cancer. Not long after, teachers approached me to start a fundraiser for our supposed trip to China to adopt triplets—a plan that existed only in Akila's imagination.

At the time, I didn't understand confabulation but knew punishment and lectures weren't effective in curbing her "lying." I asked the school team to email me any untrue stories she told them, and I began keeping a file of these instances. One staff member was shocked that I would document such things. I explained that the file was to protect not only our family and the staff involved but also Akila. She would suffer the most if a CPS investigation didn't go well.

During the IEP meeting, the new school psychologist sitting next to me listened as I explained Akila's habit of confabulating. Toward the end of the meeting, he asked, "So you don't live in a 12-bedroom mansion with a tennis court and a pool?" I laughed and explained that we lived in a small, three-bedroom house in Minneapolis. Akila had already "snowed" him with her creative storytelling.

How to handle a false allegation

When we faced our first false allegation, we were still figuring things out, but somehow, I instinctively knew how to respond. What many parents do in these situations is get angry with the child, emphasizing how much trouble they could have caused. They may say things like, "You could have got us into serious trouble" or, "You could have been placed in foster care, and your siblings taken away." Unfortunately, this approach can backfire by giving the child an idea of how to retaliate in the future when they're upset.

Instead, I recommend avoiding questions like, "Did you say that?" These only set the child up to lie or confabulate further. Instead, ask open-ended, non-confrontational questions. When Akila made a false allegation, I asked her, "Do those things really happen in our family?" She said no. I replied, "I'm so relieved, because I didn't think they did." Then, I explained how statements like that could have unintended consequences. I told her, "When you tell other students that Mom and Dad abuse you, they'll tell their parents and the staff. No one will let their kids come to our house for a playdate or birthday party, and they probably won't invite you to their house either."

She was stunned by this information. I continued, "I would never let you go to someone's house if I thought their parents were abusive." It was a shocking realization for her and made her more aware of how such untruths could impact her socially. While this didn't guarantee she wouldn't make similar statements in the future, it significantly reduced the likelihood.

Working with investigators

When dealing with an investigator, the key is to remain calm and present the facts. Educate them about confabulation and provide examples of your child's other fabricated stories in a variety of settings including home, school, neighbors, etc. This helps them understand the context and your child's neurological tendencies. In most cases, these investigations result in better supports and services for the child, as they bring attention to the need for additional resources.

Finally, connect with other caregivers who have experienced similar situations. You're not alone, and hearing from others who understand can provide valuable insight and reassurance. By staying calm, documenting behaviors, and working collaboratively with professionals, you can navigate these challenges while protecting and supporting your child.

The impact of early misunderstandings

I can't help but feel bummed that we didn't understand confabulation earlier in Akila's life. It wasn't until high school that we learned about it. By that point, we'd spent 16 years trying to "catch her" in lies, calling her a liar, and telling her she was untrustworthy.

Looking back, I wonder how many rages we could have avoided if we'd had this understanding sooner. How many of those rages were triggered simply because we didn't grasp that her "lies" were actually symptoms of her brain injury? I don't dwell in guilt—I've learned to move forward. But these experiences fuel my passion for educating others. If I can help even one family avoid the mistakes we made, it will all be worth it.

Chapter 9

Sticky Fingers: Understanding Stealing Through a New Lens

Stealing and the abstract concept of ownership

Not all individuals with fetal alcohol spectrum disorder (FASD) will struggle with stealing. Just like aggression, stealing is one of many symptoms that varies widely across the spectrum. To paraphrase a saying used for people with neurodivergence, "If you've met one person with FASD, you've met one person with FASD." While there are commonalities, each individual's experience is unique.

Stealing is often tied to deficits in *impulse control*, one of the brain functions frequently impacted by prenatal alcohol exposure. Many individuals with FASD may also struggle with the *abstract concept of ownership*, particularly those with lower IQs or intellectual disabilities, though this challenge is not limited to those populations. For some, understanding ownership is a lifelong struggle.

For example, I once took an 11-year-old child we were providing respite care for to a big-box store to purchase a few items. As we walked through the aisles, this child noticed a stuffed animal on a shelf with a price tag displayed underneath it. She understood that it was for sale and that we needed to pay for it before taking it home. However, a little later, we came across a stuffed animal lying on the floor with a tag still attached. To her, this seemed different. Since it wasn't displayed on a shelf with a price listed next to it, she believed it was free to take.

This incident highlights the *concrete thinking* that is common for individuals with FASD. They often struggle to generalize rules and may view each situation in isolation. Without clear, consistent boundaries and explanations, their understanding of concepts like ownership can remain fragmented and inconsistent.

Understanding that stealing is often a symptom of a brain-based disability rather than willful disobedience helps caregivers approach these situations with patience and empathy. With the right strategies and support, many individuals with FASD can develop a stronger understanding of these concepts over time.

The impact of misunderstanding

When Akila began stealing, we were embarrassed. We felt judged by those around us—teachers, neighbors, family members—and assumed they blamed us as parents. This shame and frustration drove us to use punitive measures, like the infamous incident where we threw away her beloved blankie. Even after her FASD diagnosis, we didn't yet understand the disability's full implications.

We entered parenting with a certain level of arrogance, I'm ashamed to admit. Between babysitting friends' children, caring for our nieces and nephews, and my professional experience working with teenagers, we felt well prepared. Even my accountant husband had a natural rapport with kids. We thought, *This is going to be a breeze.* Our plan was simple: be loving, firm, strict, and consistent. We were confident we'd rock this parenting gig.

Then nothing worked, and we had some serious humble pie thrown in our faces.

It took years for us to truly understand how Akila's brain injury impacted her. I started attending workshops and reading books, but even then, practical strategies to better support her were hard to come by. Early on, we were fortunate to attend a training led by Kari Fletcher, an extraordinary caregiver based in Minnesota. Kari is one of the most gifted practitioners of connected relational parenting I've ever met. I've learned more from her than any other professional, and I will always be grateful for the wisdom she shared.

Shifting the paradigm

Once we reframed stealing as a symptom of Akila's brain injury, we addressed it differently. We sat her down and said, "We understand now that stealing is part of your brain injury. We won't be mad at you for stealing, and we won't punish you for it. But we will talk about it each time it happens because stealing can get you in trouble in the world, and we want to help you learn."

This shift created an entirely different dynamic.

Not long after that conversation, Akila stole a cell phone. I brought the phone to her and asked, "Who do I need to return this to?" Her response? "That's the school superintendent's phone."

I had to excuse myself to laugh in private and text a few of the teachers I had got to know well. The idea of Akila stealing his phone was almost comical, especially given our collective dislike for this superintendent. After regaining my composure, I returned and asked her where the phone had been when she took it. She explained how she loved visiting the school district office secretaries during lunch, and on this particular day, no one was there, but the district office door was unlocked, and his phone was on his desk.

Walking through the process

I asked her what she felt when she first saw the phone.

"I got really excited," she admitted.

"What happened next?"

"I grabbed it."

"How did it feel to hold the phone?"

"It felt really good, Mom, because I've wanted a cell phone my whole life."

I gently asked how she thought the superintendent and secretaries felt about the missing phone, and if whoever left the door unlocked maybe got into trouble. I asked how she felt now about taking the phone.

"Not good."

"Why?" I asked.

"Because it wasn't mine, and that's stealing."

For years, therapy sessions had focused on teaching Akila to tell the nearest adult when she felt the urge to take something. On rare occasions, she did this successfully. I had gone to everyone in her school, including janitors cafeteria staff, secretaries, and teachers, and told them all that if Akila ever came up to them and said she felt like taking something, they should tell her how proud of her they were and should take her to the office to process it with someone.

"What should you have done when you saw the phone?" I asked.

"I should have told the closest adult," she said.

"Why didn't you?"

I should have been prepared for her response but it took me by surprise: "Mom, I told you, there weren't any adults there."

This was a pivotal moment. Akila wasn't intentionally defying us—her brain simply couldn't navigate the problem. She was stuck in a rigid, concrete thought process and couldn't figure out how to manage the situation without an immediate adult present. We believed our strategy was concrete enough, but time and time again, she found gaps in what we thought were solid plans.

The power of connection

Previously, we had asked her the same questions when she had stolen things, but the answers were always, "I don't know" or, "I don't want to talk about it." We were finally starting to understand that punitive approaches escalated her anxiety. She would fixate on the punishment, fearing our disappointment and frustration. Now, with a connected approach, the absence of fear allowed her to engage in a meaningful discussion.

Though this wasn't the last time Akila stole something, I'm proud to say that after about a year and a half of using this approach, she stopped stealing entirely. She hasn't stolen anything since she was about 13 years old.

Stop signs: A creative strategy for managing impulse control

We provided respite care for a teenage girl with FASD (let's call her Suzie), who struggled with taking items from our bathroom—hygiene products, makeup, and other small objects. Every time her parents came to pick her up, we would go through her bags to see what "extra" items might have found their way in. Without fail, we'd find several things that didn't belong to her.

In an effort to address this, I decided to try a new strategy. I started placing stop signs and personalized notes in the bathroom drawers and cabinets where these items were kept. Each note included her name and a simple message, such as, "Suzie, Stop!" along with a paper stop sign.

For this particular teenager, the visual reminders worked remarkably well. The stop signs helped her pause and think before impulsively taking something. It was a small, simple intervention that significantly reduced the behavior.

Why it worked

1. **Visual cues:** Many individuals with FASD respond well to visual reminders because they are concrete and immediate. A stop sign is a universally recognized signal that prompts a person to halt and reconsider their actions.

2. **Personalization:** Including her name on the notes made the intervention feel more direct and specific, increasing its impact.

3. **Immediate feedback:** The signs provided an in-the-moment reminder, which is critical for individuals with FASD who often struggle with delayed consequences or remembering rules.

4. **Relationship building and non-shaming:** I very intentionally spoke with Suzie about the signs and let her know I wasn't mad and that she wasn't bad, but that the signs were just a reminder for her to not take things. We agreed on a deal where at the end of her respite, I would always send one item home with her which we would choose together.

Limitations and adaptations

While this strategy was effective for Suzie, it's important to note that not every individual with FASD will respond to visual cues in the same way. For some, a stop sign might be ignored or even trigger defiance. As with all strategies, it's about trial and error, adapting to what works for the individual.

If this approach doesn't work, consider experimenting with other types of visual reminders or strategies:

- **Positive reinforcement notes:** Instead of "Stop!" try a message like, "Thank you for asking before taking this."
- **Locking cabinets:** If visual reminders aren't effective, physical barriers like locks might be necessary.
- **Enlist their help:** If something is missing, enlist the help of the child with FASD in finding the item. Do not accuse them of taking it, even if you know they did.

The stop sign strategy is a great example of how small, thoughtful interventions can make a big difference in managing challenging behaviors. It's worth trying with individuals who struggle with impulse control, especially when paired with other relational and supportive strategies. Sometimes, the simplest solutions are the most effective!

Prevention is key

As I have stated, when Akila was younger we initially tried to address her stealing by using consequences but we did eventually realize she wasn't stealing out of malice or defiance—she simply couldn't control the impulse. It became clear that her brain wasn't wired to respond to traditional discipline in this area. Once we recognized this, we shifted our focus from punishment to prevention, working hard to minimize her opportunities to steal as much as possible.

One of our first steps was to purchase a gun safe to lock up items like car keys, wallets, and other important belongings. These items frequently went missing, and securing them helped reduce the stress and frustration for everyone in the house. I also got a lockbox for my makeup to keep in the bathroom, as it would often disappear. Over time, lockboxes became a staple in our home. We even bought one for each child, including Akila, so everyone had a safe place to keep their personal and precious belongings.

During this time, Akila went through a brief but stressful phase of stealing from stores. When this happened, we made sure to keep a close eye on her during shopping trips—and we tried to avoid taking her to stores whenever possible. Before leaving the store, we would check her pockets to make sure she hadn't taken anything. We always did this in a way that wasn't shaming or accusatory. Instead, we framed it as part of our routine to help her stay safe and avoid trouble.

We took similar precautions when visiting friends or family. Before leaving, we would quietly check Akila's pockets to ensure nothing had been taken. I vividly remember one holiday celebration at Michael's brother's house. After an enjoyable evening, we packed the kids into the mini-van to head home. Before we could leave, Michael's sister-in-law came out to check Akila for stolen items. She even checked to see if Akila had layered extra clothing or undergarments under her own, as she had done several times before. While some might have found this offensive or intrusive, I thought it was incredibly thoughtful and practical. She understood Akila's challenges and approached the situation with care and without judgment, which meant the world to me.

At school, a similar system was in place. At the end of each day, a teaching assistant would discreetly check Akila's backpack and pockets to make sure nothing extra had been taken. If they found something, they would simply remove it without making a big deal about it or embarrassing her. Occasionally, we would have conversations with her about these incidents, but we didn't do this every time. By then, we had learned that lectures didn't deter her stealing and often made her feel more overwhelmed and frustrated. Instead, we focused on prevention and creating a safe environment where she could thrive.

These strategies required effort and vigilance, but they also brought us peace of mind. More importantly, they helped Akila feel supported rather than punished. We came to understand that her stealing wasn't about disobedience; it was about impulse control, something she struggled with deeply. By putting systems in place to prevent these behaviors, we reduced stress for everyone and created an environment where Akila could feel more secure. Prevention wasn't just about managing her behavior—it was about helping her navigate the world in a way that felt safe and manageable for her.

Building an effective approach

Connected relational parenting strategies are transformative for children and adolescents with FASD—or any individual with neurodivergence or a history of trauma. These strategies emphasize connection, understanding, and collaboration, rather than punishment. When I train caregivers or professionals, I suggest that they use these strategies with all children.

If there's one thing I've learned, it's this: while traditional strategies may work for neurotypical kids, they can harm neurodivergent children by escalating anxiety and damaging relationships. When we parent through connection, we create space for trust, growth, and genuine learning. And that's the real win—not just for our kids, but for us as caregivers too. I fully believe these strategies should be used with all kids.

Chapter 10

Family Ties: Siblings and Building Strong Relationships

Sibling support

Growing up with a sibling with fetal alcohol spectrum disorder (FASD) can be deeply challenging. The experiences my other children endured and witnessed were often extreme. Watching a sibling become aggressive toward a parent is both traumatic and stressful for a developing child or adolescent. Caregivers and professionals must be proactive in providing support for siblings, recognizing their unique experiences and the toll it takes on their well-being.

Equal and fair

It's also essential to teach our children the difference between equal and fair. Children and adolescents are often obsessed with fairness. When I worked in middle schools, I felt as if I heard the word "fair" about 100 times a day. One way we helped our kids understand this concept was by using a simple visual graphic illustrating the difference between equal and fair.

In the graphic, we explained that equal means everyone gets the same thing, while fair means everyone gets what they need to succeed. This concept highlights that, because of our brain differences, we all require varying levels of support in different areas. While it may not look fair, it's actually what each person needs—it's just not equal.

I remember once when a personal care attendant was taking Akila bowling, my youngest son, Zeke, was upset and said, "It's not fair." I asked him, "When was the last time Akila was invited to a birthday party or a playdate?" He paused and realized he couldn't think of a time. I explained that Akila needed these extra opportunities for social interaction because she didn't get them in the same way he did. It was fair, even though it wasn't equal. He was able to understand, and it helped him reframe his perspective.

Helping children grasp this distinction can prevent resentment among siblings and foster empathy for the unique challenges and needs of everyone in the family. It's not always an easy concept to teach, but when children understand the reasoning behind certain decisions, they're more likely to accept them.

Helping kids feel seen and understood

Many children and adolescents with FASD often feel out of place, as though they don't belong in the world around them. These feelings can be overwhelming, potentially leading to depression or low self-esteem, and are sometimes expressed to their caregivers. One effective way to address this is by normalizing their brain differences, helping them understand that their challenges are part of who they are and that they are not alone in their experiences.

A strategy I recommend to families is to openly talk about everyone's brains—their strengths and their areas of growth. In our family, for instance, it's well known that I'm terrible at math but a quick problem-solver when numbers aren't involved. My husband, on the other hand, is a math wizard but tends to overthink, which can slow him down in other problem-solving scenarios. By having these conversations openly, we normalize the idea that everyone's brains work differently, and we all have unique strengths and areas where we need support.

It's essential to include the entire family in these discussions—parents, siblings, and anyone who plays a significant role in the child's life. This approach helps create an environment where everyone feels seen and understood. When siblings hear that their strengths and challenges are valued equally, it can foster empathy and patience for their brother or sister with FASD. Similarly, when caregivers openly acknowledge their own areas of growth, it models humility and reinforces the idea that no one is perfect.

This kind of inclusive dialogue can also help shift the focus away from what the child with FASD "can't" do and instead celebrate what they *can* do. It creates a family culture of acceptance and support, where differences are not only acknowledged but actually appreciated. This can be a powerful tool in building self-esteem and resilience, not only for the child with FASD but for the entire family.

The need for balance

When Akila's behaviors were at their most intense, she consumed almost all of our energy and attention. We reached a point where we often separated her from the other children just to keep the household manageable. For example, we would have the three other kids playing together in the family room while Akila stayed in the living room with us. While this approach helped us keep the peace, it inadvertently shortchanged the time and attention we gave the other children.

Looking back, I wish we had done more to prioritize their needs. While we made some changes, it wasn't enough to fully mitigate the impact.

Dedicated time for siblings

One of the adjustments we made was implementing a *rotating "date night"* system with our children. Each child had their own special evening with both Mom and Dad. They got to choose an activity, pick a restaurant for dinner, and purchase a small item for around $30. These evenings became treasured moments for all of us.

During these outings, we made a conscious effort not to talk about Akila or the stresses in our home. Instead, we focused entirely on the child whose turn it was. For Akila's date nights, Michael and I often remarked that those evenings felt like glimpses of what she might have been like without her brain injury. With all our attention on her and no external stressors, her behavior was exemplary, offering us a bittersweet glimpse of her potential.

In addition to date nights, Michael began taking one child with him on Saturday morning errands, giving them one-on-one time. We also created small, special moments like *late-night movie nights* for the other three children. After putting everyone to bed, we'd sneak the other kids out, once Akila was asleep, to watch a movie. This gave them a sense of exclusivity and something to look forward to. Keeping Akila up past her bedtime and messing with her routine was something we rarely did as this could cause significant behaviors for several days.

These efforts, while small, helped to ensure that our other children felt valued and seen. They also created positive memories during a time when much of their childhood was filled with the stress and chaos of managing Akila's behaviors.

It's essential to acknowledge that siblings of children with FASD often carry unique burdens. They may feel neglected, overly responsible, or even resentful. Proactively supporting them—through dedicated time, open communication, and programs tailored to their needs—can make a significant difference in their emotional and psychological well-being. These moments of connection not only strengthen sibling relationships but also help preserve a sense of normalcy in an otherwise challenging environment.

Sibling-specific programs

One of the structured programs we tried was Sibshops, which was developed in 1982 to support siblings of children with special needs. Many children's hospital systems around the world offer Sibshops, including the hospital we used. When the opportunity came up, I signed up all three of my other kids.

After the program, I asked Imani, our oldest, what she thought. She said it was "okay," but I could tell she felt uncomfortable. When I encouraged her to elaborate, she shared that it felt awkward. The group participants were going around the circle, sharing their experiences. One child said their sibling was having heart surgery, another shared that their sibling had cancer. When it was my children's turn, they had to share that their sister hits their mom and calls her a "fucking bitch." Imani described it as a classic *Sesame Street* moment: "One of these things is not like the others." Their issues just didn't fit within the medical challenges the other children were facing.

A better fit: Kidshops

After this experience, I connected with our local NAMI (National Alliance on Mental Illness) chapter, a U.S.-based organization. NAMI had developed a version of Sibshops called Kidshops, specifically tailored for siblings of children with mental health or behavioral challenges. My kids attended this program and found it to be a much better fit. The focus was finally on them, and they felt comfortable sharing and discussing their experiences without the disconnect they had felt in the medical-oriented Sibshops.

Kidshops gave my children the opportunity to process and discuss the unique challenges of growing up with a sibling like Akila. It was a space where they didn't feel judged or out of place, and that made a world of difference for their emotional well-being. Programs like this are crucial for siblings, as they allow them to feel understood and provide them with tools to cope with the complexities of their family dynamics.

Protecting siblings from big behaviors

One of the most common concerns caregivers express is how to shield their other children from the extreme behaviors of a sibling with FASD. I vividly remember an out-of-body experience that highlighted just how much Akila's behavior was impacting my other children—and it's a memory that still feels raw.

One evening when Akila was 12, I was cooking dinner before Michael got home. Let me say upfront—I truly hate cooking. It has always been one of the most stressful parts of parenting for me, and I'm not a good cook. That night, I decided to attempt a new Asian dish, juggling several pots on the stove, including one with boiling water.

Akila came into the kitchen, wanting something I can't even recall now. Whatever it was, I couldn't accommodate her immediately because I was cooking, and that infuriated her. She escalated quickly. I tried a few distractions, but nothing worked. Suddenly, she went to grab the boiling pot of water to throw it on me. I had to act instantly, grabbing her by both wrists to stop her. This enraged her further, and she became verbally and physically aggressive, screaming threats and kicking me as I held her wrists.

My nine-year-old son, Zeke, heard the commotion and ran into the kitchen. Crying, he jumped on Akila's back and began trying to bite her, shouting over and over, "Why do you always hurt Mom?"

It was one of the most heartbreaking moments of my parenting journey.

I couldn't let go of Akila's wrists, as she was completely dysregulated, so I called for my other son, Hezekiah, to come help. He pulled Zeke off Akila, and I told them to go to our next-door neighbor's house—a trusted, grandmotherly figure to my children who was also a retired special education teacher and a mentor to me. The boys were reluctant to leave, worried about my safety, but I reassured them, "I'll be fine. This is just another night for us." Reluctantly, they went.

I then moved Akila into the living room to restrain her properly. Let me be clear: I don't advocate for physical restraints as a standard response. It's not the right fit for many of our children, and it's something we only use because we've learned that for Akila, it helps her regulate. In fact, now Akila is in her mid-twenties, the *idea* of being put in a hold is often enough to help her calm herself. But back then, it was one of the few tools we had.

While I was restraining Akila, she continued yelling hateful, hurtful things, which was typical in these moments. Meanwhile, Imani, age 11, stepped into the kitchen to take over cooking. She asked me what the next steps were for the meal. I told her to bring me the recipe book. Holding Akila down, I glanced at the book and directed Imani: "Add the peapods and then..." After handing the recipe book back to her, I had a surreal moment where I felt as if I was watching myself from the outside.

There I was, restraining my child on the floor, calmly giving cooking instructions. I had visions of the many times I had helped the kids with homework all while restraining Akila. This had become our normal. And in that moment, I realized how deeply unsustainable it was.

The unexpected support at a school open house

After the boiling water episode, it became painfully clear that we all needed a break. At 12 years old, Akila was admitted to a crisis home at our request. She stayed there for three months, beginning the week before school started. Her first night in the crisis home coincided with the back-to-school open house—a day that was devastating for our family.

Michael and I were consumed by a whirlwind of emotions: guilt, sadness, and an overwhelming sense of failure. We questioned whether we were doing the right thing, but deep down, we knew it was necessary. Akila needed a break from the chaos, and so did we.

The structured environment of the crisis home provided exactly what she needed. It allowed for adjustments to her medication and gave everyone a chance to reset. While it was one of the hardest decisions we ever made, it was a critical step toward creating a more stable and supportive dynamic at home.

For the school open houses, Michael and I divided responsibilities, each taking one or more of the other children to their respective open houses. I was walking through the halls in a daze, barely functioning. Guilt weighed heavily on me, and I was exhausted—physically, emotionally, and mentally. As I wandered aimlessly, feeling like a shell of myself, I unexpectedly ran into the mother of one of Akila's classmates.

This mother had a unique perspective that few others could offer. She had grown up with foster and adoptive siblings and had even had a brother with FASD. She and her husband had graciously taken all four of my children for a weekend of respite in the past, a rare and precious gift that I deeply appreciated.

She must have sensed my distress. When she asked how I was doing, the floodgates opened, and I broke down crying right there in the hallway. She was calm and compassionate—the exact person I needed in that moment.

She shared her memories of growing up in a household with a sibling who had FASD. She described how, as a child, she would sit in her bedroom, holding a pillow over her head to drown out the sound of her brother's rages. It was an image that hit me hard. It mirrored the experiences my other children were living through, and yet she spoke with such understanding and validation. Her words helped to relieve some of the crushing guilt I was carrying.

"You're doing the right thing," she told me, her voice steady and reassuring. Her encouragement felt like a lifeline. In a situation where I constantly felt judged or misunderstood, she was a rare person who truly understood—and who could tell me I wasn't failing, even when I felt as if I was.

There was no coincidence in that encounter; I am convinced that I was meant to run into her that night. Her compassion and validation carried me through one of the darkest moments of my parenting journey, and I will always be grateful for her kindness. Sometimes, when you're drowning, all it takes is one person to pull you up for air. That night, she was that person for me.

Code words and phrases for crisis situations

Using code words or phrases can be a lifesaver for families navigating the challenges of big behaviors. These simple tools help keep communication calm, discreet, and effective during stressful situations, especially when emotions are running high.

Code words for siblings

When a child is dysregulated, it's often unrealistic to expect them to remove themselves from the environment. Instead, families can use a code word to signal the other children to step away and create a calmer space. If you have a child who will go to their room when they are dysregulated or just want to be left alone, this is a gift!

For a while, our family used the code word *"pineapple."* If Michael or I said "pineapple," it meant the other children were to immediately go to their rooms because things were about to get chaotic. Over time, we refined this into a crisis plan where the other kids would go to a neighbor's house when Akila's behaviors escalated.

It's perfectly fine to incentivize siblings for their cooperation. When they responded to the code word and moved out of harm's way, we often rewarded them with something special. They absolutely deserved it for handling these moments with maturity and understanding.

Code phrases for parents

In two-parent households, a code phrase can be just as valuable for maintaining unity and composure. For instance, there were times when either Michael or I would get drawn into a power struggle with Akila or one of the other kids. It's easy to lose sight of the bigger picture in the heat of the moment, and when one of us would step in to interrupt, it often felt embarrassing and undermining.

To address this, we came up with a discreet code phrase: *"I forgot to tell you, we're almost out of milk."* When one of us used this phrase, it signaled to the other to stop engaging, take a step back, and allow the other parent to take over. It was a subtle way to "tag out" without making the situation more volatile or losing face in front of the kids.

For single-parent families

Unfortunately, tagging out isn't an option for single-parent families. However, single caregivers can still use code words to alert children to safety plans, or they can have prearranged signals with trusted friends, neighbors, or family members to provide backup when things get difficult. Having a support system in place is invaluable in these moments.

Code words and phrases are simple, but their impact can be profound. They help prevent escalation, protect relationships, and maintain a sense of control and calm during crises. Whether you're signaling the siblings to retreat or giving yourself permission to step out of a power struggle, these tools can make a challenging situation a little more manageable.

A brother's love: Zeke and Akila's bond

When Zeke was in high school and the only child still living at home, Akila came for an evening visit with her boyfriend, Mowgli. Mowgli and Akila have been dating since they were 18, and though they're the same age, Mowgli has expressed many times that he wants us to adopt him. While we obviously can't do that since they're dating, he has become like a fifth child to us, calling us "Mom" and "Dad" and truly feeling like part of the family.

That evening, Akila had a severe rage episode. At one point, she began chasing Mowgli around the house. I was trying to help her de-escalate, but her rage was intense and beyond what I could manage alone. Michael came downstairs to assist, but we couldn't get her to calm down. To keep Mowgli safe, we asked him to lock himself in the bathroom while we worked to get Akila regulated.

Unfortunately, my own physical limitations prevented me from restraining Akila due to ongoing back issues, so Michael stepped in. Zeke, who had been upstairs in his room, heard the commotion. He came downstairs without hesitation to help. Together, Michael and Zeke gently restrained Akila until she began to calm down. When she finally stopped physically fighting, she collapsed on the floor, sobbing.

What happened next was one of the most beautiful moments I've ever witnessed as a mother. Zeke, without any instruction, lay down beside her on the floor. Instead of chastising or scolding her, he spoke softly and lovingly, offering words of encouragement. He reminded her that she was loved, that it wasn't her fault, and that he was there for her. In that moment, Zeke showed an extraordinary level of empathy, patience, and compassion.

Later that evening, Zeke recorded an emotional video and shared it on Instagram. In the video, he spoke candidly about his experiences with Akila and her FASD. Tears streamed down his face as he shared how hard her life is, how much he loves her, and how proud he is of the person she is despite the challenges she faces. He also acknowledged the toll it has taken on our family, noting how his parents are getting older and less physically capable of handling the big behaviors, but his focus remained on Akila's strengths and her resilience.

It was a proud mama moment for me—watching my son embody such love and understanding in the face of such challenges. It reminded me that while growing up with a sibling with FASD is incredibly hard, it also fosters a deep sense of compassion and maturity that is truly remarkable.

Marriage and relationships

Raising children with disabilities, especially FASD, is an enormous challenge, and it can strain all kinds of relationships—marriages, partnerships, friendships, and connections with extended family. The unique demands and complexities of raising children with FASD often push caregivers to their limits, and this can lead to misunderstandings, frustration, and emotional distance within relationships.

Differences in parenting approaches

One of the most common struggles in two-parent households is the difficulty of getting on and staying on the same page about parenting strategies. Typical parenting techniques are often ineffective for children with FASD, but it usually takes families a long time to realize this and adjust. For those of you at the beginning of your journey—especially if your children are still young—I envy you.

If we had known then what we know now, we would have done so many things differently. My hope is that by sharing my mistakes, your journey will be smoother and more effective.

In many families, one parent is the primary caregiver. This dynamic can lead to additional challenges, as the primary caregiver often becomes the main target of the child's big behaviors. Here's why:

1. **Unrealistic expectations:** The primary caregiver is often the one who provides for the child's tangible needs—purchasing clothing, food, toys, and gifts. Many children with FASD struggle to understand the value of items or the limitations of money, leading to unrealistic expectations of the caregiver. When these expectations aren't met, it can result in anger or resentment directed at the primary caregiver.

2. **Time together:** The primary caregiver usually spends more time with the child, making them a natural focal point for the child's frustrations, anxieties, and dysregulation.

3. **Safe person effect:** Children with FASD often save their biggest behaviors for their "safe person." This is the individual they feel most comfortable expressing their emotions with, which can sometimes take the form of raging, physical aggression, or verbal outbursts.

Frustration in the secondary role

In many cases, the secondary caregiver—whether that's a father, mother, or another caregiver—may mistakenly believe that the primary caregiver is being too lenient or permissive. They may assume that stricter boundaries and harsher consequences would resolve the behaviors. My husband initially thought this when Akila was younger. However, as her behaviors escalated and became directed at him as well, as she got older, he began to see that leniency wasn't the issue—it was her brain.

Knowledge gap between partners

The primary caregiver is often the one diving deep into learning about FASD, reading books, attending support groups, going to therapy appointments, and advocating for the child. This immersion gives them a better understanding of the strategies that work. Unfortunately, it can take much longer for the secondary caregiver to reach this same level of understanding.

This knowledge gap can lead to frustration on both sides:

- **For the primary caregiver:** It's exhausting to feel as if you're carrying the entire mental and emotional load alone, especially when your partner seems resistant to new strategies.
- **For the secondary caregiver:** It can feel overwhelming or even alienating to be told that your instincts or traditional parenting approaches aren't effective.

A strategy for bridging the gap

One approach I often recommend to families is to ask your partner to attend two FASD-specific trainings, read a book, or listen to a few podcast episodes as a gift. Frame it as what you want most for your birthday, Valentine's Day, or another occasion. However, you must be very thoughtful in selecting the resources. If the chosen material isn't engaging or doesn't resonate, your partner is unlikely to try again.

Here are a few tips for selecting resources:

1. **Start with something short and accessible:** A podcast episode or short training can be less intimidating than committing to a full book or multi-day workshop.

2. **Focus on relatable content:** Choose resources that include real-life stories or examples they can connect with, preferably by an experienced caregiver, not a professional. This will hit home more effectively.

3. **Pick something that matches their personality:** If your partner values research, pick a data-driven resource. If they prefer storytelling, choose something that emphasizes personal narratives.

4. **Follow up positively:** After they've completed the resource, discuss it in a non-judgmental way. Ask what they thought or if anything stood out to them, rather than immediately pushing for changes.

Supporting each other as a team

Navigating life with a child with FASD is one of the most challenging experiences a family can face. It's essential for both caregivers to find ways to work as a team, even when they have different learning curves or perspectives. Relationships thrive when partners make space for each other's growth, frustrations, and strengths.

By staying curious, patient, and open to learning, caregivers can support not only their children but also their partnerships. Strong teamwork ultimately leads to better outcomes for everyone in the family.

Chapter 11

Your Tribe Awaits: Finding Your People

Find your people

Caring for a child with fetal alcohol spectrum disorder (FASD) can be incredibly isolating. Many caregivers start to feel as if they're losing their minds. The typical parenting strategies that work for other children don't work for theirs. Well-meaning friends, family members, and even professionals offer advice that consistently fails to address the unique challenges of FASD.

When caregivers share stories about their experiences, they're often met with responses like, "Oh, my child does that too!" While these comments are usually meant to empathize, they often leave caregivers feeling more misunderstood. People don't realize that the challenges faced by children with FASD are fundamentally different, often more extreme, and rooted in a brain injury.

The difference is in the intensity. Here's an example. When Akila was about nine or ten years old, I told a social worker how she would have explosive rages if we were out of her favorite cereal. The social worker responded, "Oh, my child does the same thing." I pushed up my sleeve to reveal the bruises from Akila's latest rage and asked, "Do you get bruised like this when your child doesn't get their favorite cereal?" That ended the comparison.

Another family I've worked with had a son who urinated around the house—but not in the toilet. When the mother shared this with a friend, the friend casually responded, "Oh, my child did that too." The mother explained that her son urinated in heating vents, drinking glasses, closets, and even on the couch. The friend fell silent.

While well-intentioned, comparing neurotypical behaviors to those of a child with FASD isn't helpful—it minimizes the challenges and leaves caregivers feeling even more isolated. What caregivers need isn't comparison; it's understanding.

I'll never forget something a friend said to me years ago when I shared some of Akila's most difficult behaviors: "Barb, how are you going to survive your life?" That blunt acknowledgment meant more to me than any comparison ever could. It validated how hard my situation was without dismissing it (and by the way, I found a way to survive and thrive—and you can too!).

Social isolation and community disconnect

The intensity of raising a child with FASD often leads families to withdraw from social events, community activities, and even family gatherings. This happens for a variety of reasons:

1. **Embarrassment and big behaviors:** When children with FASD have meltdowns or exhibit challenging behaviors in public, it can be deeply embarrassing for both the child and their caregiver. Rather than risk such an incident, many families choose to stay home.

2. **Overstimulation and routine disruption:** Community events often involve loud noises, bright lights, and unpredictable schedules—all of which can be overwhelming for children with FASD. For many, even minor disruptions to their

routine, like staying up past bedtime, can trigger a ripple effect of dysregulation that lasts for days or even weeks.

3. **Social challenges:** Many children with FASD struggle to navigate social interactions. They might feel out of place at events or simply not want to attend, leading families to miss out on social opportunities.

For these reasons, many families with children who have FASD make significant adjustments to their lives. They may leave events early to preserve routines, opt out of activities altogether, or avoid overstimulating environments. This can feel isolating, but it's often necessary to create a more stable, manageable environment for their child.

The isolation is real, but so is the resilience of these families. Recognizing the unique challenges they face—and offering genuine empathy instead of comparisons—can go a long way in supporting them. Sometimes, simply acknowledging, "I can't imagine how hard this must be," is the most meaningful thing you can say.

Grief and loss for the child

Imagine cherishing a holiday like Christmas and holding fond memories of family traditions—only to find that, due to your child's needs, you can no longer attend celebrations at your parent's house. Or, if you can attend, you must leave after just an hour and a half to avoid a meltdown. The grief and loss our kids experience due to their disability are immense. Their caregivers, too, face significant grief and loss as their lives and traditions are shaped by the realities of FASD.

Any diagnosis of a disability or disease carries an element of grief and loss. For individuals with FASD, this can be especially profound because the disability often intersects with other significant losses. Many children with FASD are part of adoptive or foster families, which means they are already processing the grief and trauma of not being with their first family. This separation, whether voluntary or involuntary, is a loss that must be acknowledged and addressed.

Caregivers play a vital role in helping children navigate these complex emotions, particularly as they come to understand their diagnosis. Recognizing and validating their feelings is an important part of helping them heal.

Telling your child about their diagnosis

I firmly believe that once caregivers have come to terms with an FASD diagnosis, they should share it with their child. We told Akila about her diagnosis shortly after she was diagnosed at age six, and it has always been a part of her narrative. Over the years, our conversations about it evolved, with explanations tailored to her developmental age and her ability to understand.

Caregivers often worry about how their child will react to this information. Anger, sadness, or feelings of injustice are all common responses, but they are natural parts of the grieving process. The key is to ensure that the child doesn't get stuck in any one stage, like anger. Caregivers should help them process these feelings and emphasize that their diagnosis doesn't define their worth or potential.

A fish out of water

Our kids often feel like fish out of water in most settings. They are square pegs in round holes, and as they grow older, many become acutely aware of this. Without support, this awareness can have a significant impact on their self-esteem.

It's critical to help them understand that being different is not only okay—it's a strength. I often tell Akila, "Normal is boring. Our family is super cool, and your brain injury is your superpower." These affirmations help her feel valued and unique, even as she navigates the challenges of her diagnosis.

By normalizing their differences, highlighting their strengths, and building connections that celebrate their individuality, we can help children with FASD embrace who they are and find their place in the world.

Appreciating honesty from professionals

Over the years, we've worked with many professionals who presented themselves as experts, even when they clearly didn't understand FASD. I get it—no one wants to admit they don't know how to help. But the professionals I've respected the most were the ones who admitted their gaps in knowledge and were open to learning.

One psychologist once told me, "I don't know a lot about FASD, but I'd love to learn from you." That humility and willingness to collaborate meant more to me than any sticker chart ever could.

Grief and loss for the caregiver

Caregivers of children with FASD often experience grief and loss, and this manifests differently at various stages of their parenting journey. While there's an initial wave of grief and loss following the diagnosis, it doesn't just end there. It has a way of creeping back into their lives when they least expect it, often triggered by specific situations, milestones, or unmet expectations. In the online coaching program where I work, we frequently help caregivers recognize when grief and loss are resurfacing. Caregivers will share challenges happening in their family, and one of us coaches will point out that it sounds like grief and loss may have crept back in.

When most people think about grief and loss, they associate it with death. However, grief is a circular process—it doesn't follow a straight line. The stages of grief, such as denial, anger, bargaining, depression, and acceptance, can arise at different points in life, often catching caregivers off guard. Having someone to help you recognize when you're in one of these stages is crucial.

Our children with FASD often express their longing to just be "normal," and caregivers share in this longing. This unfulfilled desire is a source of ongoing grief. Many families lose friends because of the challenges their children face. Family relationships are also deeply affected, and in some cases, these relationships are lost altogether. I recently worked with a family who was told by their extended family not to bring their adopted children to a Christmas gathering because only "blood" relatives were invited. Imagine the pain of receiving such a request.

In my own experience, I had a brother who blew up at my dysregulated daughter on Thanksgiving one year. He was so frustrated that he threatened to punch her in the face. While I love my brother, that was the last Thanksgiving we spent at his home, and our relationship never fully recovered.

Altered traditions and social life

Holidays and family celebrations for families like mine are rarely like those of neurotypical families. We often couldn't play games or enjoy the activities that other families do during the holidays. Instead, we were always in survival mode, working to prevent meltdowns.

Spending time with friends was also a challenge. Constant supervision of our children meant there was little room for deep conversations or fun activities like playing cards. Finding a babysitter capable of managing Akila's needs was nearly impossible. Growing up, I watched my parents socialize and play cards with their friends every weekend, but that was not a reality for us during our child-rearing years. Now that our kids are adults and out of the house, we've been able to reclaim some of that social life, but we had to grieve its absence for decades.

Financial challenges

The financial toll of raising a child with FASD is significant and often underestimated. When Akila was younger, I couldn't work full time. The constant phone calls from school, frequent suspensions, endless doctor appointments, and the need to manage her care made it impossible. Many families are in similar situations, which can have long-term financial consequences. Not only does the lack of full-time income affect immediate finances; it also impacts retirement savings.

Even for families who had hoped to retire, many find themselves continuing to care for or financially support their adult children. The financial implications include everything from repairing damage to the home or replacing valuable items like food lost from a freezer left open, to paying for damages to a neighbor's property or covering legal fees.

Yes, raising children is expensive for all families, but the additional, unpredictable costs that come with FASD can be overwhelming. Many families end up working far beyond the years they'd planned to work because of the financial burden, or they go into significant debt.

Moving forward with love

Despite these challenges, it's important to emphasize that this isn't about complaining. We love our children and wouldn't trade them for anything. But we also need to acknowledge and validate the unique grief and loss that caregivers of children with FASD face. By recognizing these realities, we can work to build stronger supports for these families and ensure they don't feel so isolated in their journey.

Finding community

When Akila was first diagnosed, I immediately began searching for other caregivers raising children with FASD. I reached out to Proof Alliance, an organization dedicated to FASD based in Minnesota, where we lived at the time. Unfortunately, they didn't have any support groups available then, so I volunteered to lead one myself. A few years later, I was working on staff at Proof Alliance, providing support to families in similar situations.

In my role, I led support groups, attended Individualized Education Program (IEP) meetings with families, met one-on-one with caregivers, and provided training as I learned everything I could about FASD. As an adoptive parent, I also became involved with support groups for adoptive, foster, and kinship caregivers. Once I started spending time with others who truly understood the challenges of raising kids with FASD, my mental health began to improve significantly.

Before I found these support groups, I had started to feel deeply isolated. My friends raising neurotypical children, despite their best intentions, could not truly understand the unique struggles we faced. During this time, I began blogging about our journey as a way to process my emotions and connect with others. This was in the early 2000s, before Facebook and other online support options were widely available.

It was at this time that I met a woman named Kari Fletcher, who had an enormous influence on me and my husband. During one of her trainings, she mentioned that she blogged about her experiences and encouraged me to do the same. Soon, I became part of a network of caregivers who blogged, and we would read and comment on each other's posts. This early community was incredibly validating. Eventually, Facebook groups and other online forums became the go-to spaces for finding support, offering a new way to connect with others.

Through these connections, both online and in person, I slowly began to emerge from the dark hole I had fallen into. At that time in my life, I was suffering from several migraines each week. When I visited a neurologist, he told me I needed to eliminate the stress in my life. Easier said than done when raising a child with FASD.

Finding support and understanding

As I learned from other caregivers, I began to shift from being a punitive caregiver to a connected and relational one. I realized we weren't alone, and, most importantly, I started to understand that we weren't doing anything "wrong." This realization was freeing after years of feeling judged and isolated.

Sitting with others—whether online or in person—who are navigating the same chaos is empowering. It helps reduce the isolation, provides perspective by showing that others may be facing even greater struggles, and offers hope. That hope is invaluable.

In my role at Families Rising, I now train adoptive, foster, and kinship caregivers—as well as professionals—on how to lead support groups. Support groups often get a bad reputation, partly because Hollywood portrays them as cheesy or ineffective.

However, when they are led properly, they can be a lifeline for isolated caregivers.

These groups provide a safe space where caregivers can share openly without fear of judgment. They offer not only emotional support but also practical advice and strategies from those who have been there. Support groups foster a sense of belonging, a feeling that you are not alone, and a community that truly understands the complexities of raising children with FASD. When done right, they are a powerful tool for healing, growth, and resilience.

Respite: A lifeline for families

Caring for children with challenging behaviors, particularly those with FASD, can be exhausting. Respite, or planned breaks for both the child and their caregivers, is a critical tool for maintaining mental health and preventing burnout. However, accessing respite care often proves to be a significant challenge.

The challenge of finding respite

When Akila was young, our family qualified for respite care through our county. Unfortunately, despite this support, the system struggled to match us with caregivers willing and able to take her. The primary issue was the extremely low reimbursement rate, which made it difficult to find qualified people willing to take on the responsibility.

In our desperation for a break, I turned to our circle of friends. Initially, I asked close friends for help on specific weekends. Most responses were along the lines of, "I'm sorry, we're busy." I quickly realized that I needed to approach this differently.

Getting creative with respite requests

I reached out to acquaintances I saw only occasionally—friends from high school, past co-workers, or neighbors we no longer saw regularly. Instead of asking for help on a particular weekend, I asked if they could take Akila sometime in the next six months. Framing the request this way gave them the flexibility to choose a time that worked for their schedule. The response was overwhelmingly positive—everyone said yes.

Why respite worked for everyone

Respite provided a win-win situation. Akila enjoyed these breaks, often staying with people she didn't see regularly, which reduced the likelihood of behavioral challenges. When she stayed with close family or friends, her comfort level with them sometimes led to escalated behaviors. By sending her to people she wasn't as familiar with but whom we knew and trusted, we found that she generally stayed regulated.

The benefits extended beyond Akila. Her siblings, who often bore the brunt of the stress at home, thrived during respite weekends. On the first night, we would allow them to have a friend sleep over—a simple joy that was hard to manage when Akila was home. The second night, we focused on family activities, creating moments of connection and fun that were otherwise rare in the chaos.

For Michael and me, respite felt like a breath of fresh air. It allowed us to recharge and gave us the space to focus on our other children, our marriage, and ourselves. These breaks were invaluable in helping us regain the patience and perspective we needed to continue parenting Akila effectively.

Respite tips for families

1. **Be flexible with timing:** Instead of asking for a specific date, ask for availability within a broader timeframe. This increases the likelihood that someone will say yes.

2. **Consider unconventional helpers:** Reach out to friends or acquaintances you don't see often. They may be more willing to help than you think, especially if the request is planned well in advance.

3. **Value the break for everyone:** Respite is not just for the caregivers—it's also for the child with FASD and their siblings. Everyone benefits from a change in routine and environment.

4. **Advocate for better respite services:** Advocate for improved support systems, including better reimbursement rates for respite providers. Families like ours depend on these services to prevent caregiver burnout.

5. Be sure to provide them with the right info about FASD and the do's and don'ts specific to your child.

Respite is not just a luxury, it's a necessity for families navigating the challenges of raising children with FASD or other complex needs. Finding it might require creativity, persistence, and support from unexpected places, but it can be a game-changer for maintaining balance and well-being in your family.

A turning point: Building connection over consequences

There is a caregiver I've worked with for over ten years, a mother of two children with FASD. For years, she resisted shifting to more connected, relational caregiving strategies. She was stuck in a cycle of using traditional approaches like consequences and punishments, even though they weren't working. But I will never forget the moment she had a breakthrough.

It was a Saturday afternoon in early spring in Minnesota. She called me, distressed, after a blowout with her son, who was in seventh or eighth grade at the time. During their argument, he got on his bike and rode away without permission. She was livid—and worried.

When she called, we ended up on the phone for almost two hours. As we talked, I did a mini-training session with her, sharing examples and stories like the ones in this book. I emphasized how connected relational strategies had made a big difference with Akila. I could tell she was listening intently, but I also sensed her struggle.

Her first instinct was to punish her son when he returned home. "He needs to learn that running off like that isn't acceptable," she said. I asked her if, in the past, punishment had helped prevent similar behaviors. She admitted it hadn't.

"So why keep doing it?" I asked gently.

I explored with her why punishment and consequences often don't work for kids with FASD—concepts I've covered earlier in this book. Slowly, I could feel her perspective starting to shift. She asked, "Then what do I say to him when he gets home?"

I suggested something simple: "When he comes back, just say, 'I'm so glad you're home safe. I was worried about you.' And if he's open to it, give him a hug."

She was quiet for a moment, then said, "Okay. I'll try it."

Several hours later, she texted me. "I said what you suggested," she wrote, "and he broke down crying. We ended up having a really good conversation. I can't believe it worked."

That day was a turning point for her. For years, she had been resistant to changing her strategies, but this experience showed her the power of connection over correction. From that point on, she began to shift how she and her husband approached parenting their son. The results were remarkable. Her relationship with her son improved significantly, and she became his biggest advocate as he transitioned into young adulthood.

Key takeaways

- **Reassess what isn't working:** If a strategy isn't producing the desired results, it's worth questioning why and exploring alternatives. Punishment often fails with kids who have FASD because their brains process situations differently.

- **Lead with connection:** A simple statement like "I'm glad you're safe" can open the door to meaningful conversations. Connection fosters trust and reduces the child's anxiety, creating space for growth and understanding.

- **Breakthroughs are possible:** Even if you've been resistant to change or feel stuck in old habits, it's never too late to shift your approach. Small changes in how we respond can lead to big transformations.

This story is a powerful reminder that when we focus on building relationships rather than enforcing consequences, we create an environment where healing and growth can take root.

A hard-learned lesson: Shifting from punishment to connection

One of the families I worked with had moved to a rural area to help keep their teenage boys out of trouble. The boys, adopted after their previous placements disrupted, had significant behavioral challenges and were unsafe with electronics, so they didn't have personal devices. Despite this, one of their adult siblings secretly gave them each an iPod.

After a few weeks, the parents started hearing from friends and family that the boys were active on social media. The parents tried for days to get the boys to hand over the devices, but the boys denied having them. The situation escalated one evening at dinner when the father, in frustration, told the boys to sleep in the barn without dinner as a consequence.

In the middle of the night, the boys ran away. A sheriff's deputy found them, and the parents were charged with neglect. Devastated and scared, the mother called me late on a Friday night after the boys had been removed and placed in foster care. This was my first interaction with this family.

We talked for two hours. She was heartbroken and consumed with guilt. I spent much of the conversation explaining the effects of trauma and FASD, particularly how these boys' brains worked differently. I explained the importance of never withholding basic needs like food or shelter from children, especially those who had experienced trauma.

On Monday, at the court hearing, I encouraged her to take responsibility and acknowledge their lack of training in how to parent children with such complex needs. She and her husband did just that, and they were able to get the boys back. Soon after, they moved back to the city, feeling that the rural setting wasn't providing the structure and support they needed. I started doing regular parent coaching sessions with them.

During one coaching session, the father brought up a new issue. He explained that one of the boys was constantly swearing, and no matter what he tried, he couldn't get him to stop. To address it, the father had taken the boy to a park across the street and made him run up and down a hill repeatedly as punishment. While they were there, a city police officer stopped to ask what they were doing. When the father explained, the officer praised him, saying, "Good job, Dad!" This affirmation from the officer left the father feeling good.

"What do you think about it?" he asked me.

I told him I didn't like the approach. He admitted that he thought I would say that. So I asked, "Did it work? Did he stop swearing?"

The father admitted that the boy was still swearing as much as ever. "So," I said, "it wasn't successful."

I explained that I don't have an issue with physical activity, but I don't believe in using it as a punishment. Instead, I suggested turning it into a connected, relational activity. "Why not go to the park together, run up and down the hill, and make it fun? You'd still be getting him the sensory input and exercise he needs, but you'd also be building your relationship."

The father paused, then nodded. "That makes sense," he said. "I'll try it."

Over time, this couple fully embraced connected relational parenting. They began to see improvements in their boys' behaviors and, more importantly, their relationships with them. A few years later, they reached out again—not because they needed help, but because they wanted guidance on how to educate their friends and family about trauma-informed strategies.

"Once you start using these approaches," the father said, "it's hard to go back. You want everyone to understand and use them."

Key takeaways

- **Punishment vs. connection:** Using punishments like physical activity as a consequence may seem effective in the moment, but it rarely leads to lasting behavior change. Instead, use activities to build relationships and meet sensory needs in a positive way.

- **Take responsibility and learn:** It's okay to admit when you've made mistakes in parenting. Acknowledging gaps in knowledge and seeking support can pave the way for positive change.

- **Empowering others:** Once you see the benefits of trauma-informed, connected parenting strategies, it's natural to want to share them with others. Helping friends, family, and community members understand these approaches can create a ripple effect of understanding and empathy.

Parenting kids with complex needs is a journey, but with the right mindset, tools, and willingness to learn, you can turn even the hardest moments into opportunities for growth and connection.

Hope

With the right supports, individuals living with fetal alcohol spectrum disorder can achieve incredible things. Their potential is vast, and as caregivers, educators, and advocates, it's our responsibility to nurture their strengths and provide the scaffolding they need to succeed.

Hope is a powerful force. It keeps us learning, advocating, connecting, and moving forward, even when the challenges feel overwhelming. My daughter, Akila, is my greatest teacher and my deepest inspiration. She has shown me that she is not broken—she simply learns and experiences the world differently. She is resilient, beautiful, and someone who makes me proud every single day.

One of the most important lessons I've learned is to focus on strengths. Every child, whether they have FASD or not, has unique talents and abilities. By identifying those strengths and pouring energy into developing them, we give our children a foundation for success and confidence.

I hope that each of you—whether you are caregivers, professionals, or family members—can find and celebrate the strengths in the individuals you support. By doing so, you remind them, and yourself, that they are not defined by their challenges. They are worth every effort, every sacrifice, and every ounce of love and care we can give. Hold on to hope, because it will guide you through the toughest moments and remind you of the beauty and potential in every journey.

Recommended Resources

Over 20 years ago, resources on FASD were scarce and just beginning to emerge. While more resources are available today, there is still a significant need for further education and awareness. Below, I've listed several of my favorite resources for those who want to explore and learn more about FASD.

Books

Fetal Alcohol Spectrum Disorders: Trying Differently Rather Than Harder, Diane Malbin

FASD Essential Supports: Understanding and Supporting People with Fetal Alcohol Spectrum Disorders, Nate Sheets

Making Sense of the Madness: An FASD Survival Guide, Jeff Noble

FASD Sound Bytes and Sanity Savers, Jeff Noble

Damaged Angels: An Adoptive Mother's Struggle to Understand the Tragic Toll of Alcohol in Pregnancy, Bonnie Buxton

Explained by Brain: The FASD Workbook for Parents, Carers and Educators, Vanessa Spiller

Programs

FASD Success's "Caregiver Kickstart" Online Coaching Program: http://www.fasdsuccess.com (this is a program FASD Success created and hosts)

Eileen Divine's Resilience Room: www.eileendevine.com/the-resilience-room

Podcasts

FASD Success Show
FASD Hope
FASD Family Life
Living with FASD

Websites

FASD United (U.S.-wide FASD organization): www.fasdunited.org

CanFASD (Canadian FASD organization): https://canfasd.ca

FASD Hub (UK FASD organization): www.adoptionuk.org/fasd-hub

NOFASD (Australian FASD organization): www.nofasd.org.au

Proof Alliance: www.proofalliance.org

References

Chapter 1

1 Astley Hemingway, S. J., Bledsoe, J. M., Brooks, A., Davies, J. K., *et al.* (2018). Twin study confirms virtually identical prenatal alcohol exposures can lead to markedly different fetal alcohol spectrum disorder outcomes—fetal genetics influences fetal vulnerability. *Advances in Pediatric Research*, 5(3), 23. https://doi.org/10.24105/apr.2019.5.23.

Chapter 2

1 Astley Hemingway, S. J., Bledsoe, J. M., Brooks, A., Davies, J. K., *et al.* (2018). Twin study confirms virtually identical prenatal alcohol exposures can lead to markedly different fetal alcohol spectrum disorder outcomes—fetal genetics influences fetal vulnerability. *Advances in Pediatric Research*, 5(3), 23. https://doi.org/10.24105/apr.2019.5.23.

2 Breton-Larrivée, M., Elder, E., Legault, L. M., Langford-Avelar, A., MacFarlane, A. J., & McGraw, S. (2023). Mitigating the detrimental developmental impact of early fetal alcohol exposure using a maternal methyl donor-enriched diet. *FASEB Journal: Official Publication of the Federation of American Societies for Experimental Biology*, 37(4), e22829. https://doi.org/10.1096/fj.202201564R.

3 Poggi Davis, E., Hankin, B. L., Glynn, L. M., Head, K., & Kim, D. J. (2020). Prenatal maternal stress, child cortical thickness, and adolescent depressive symptoms. *Child Development*, 91(2), e432–e450. doi: 10.1111/cdev.132522019.

4 Grizenko, N., Fortier, M. E., Zadorozny, C., Thakur, G., *et al.* (2012). Maternal stress during pregnancy, ADHD symptomatology in children and

genotype: Gene–environment interaction. *Journal of the Canadian Academy of Child and Adolescent Psychiatry*, 21(1), 9–15.

5 May, P. A., *et al.* (2018). Prevalence of Fetal Alcohol Spectrum Disorders in 4 US communities. *JAMA*, 319(5), 474–482. https://doi.org/10.1001/jama.2017.21896.

6 Maenner, M. J., Warren, Z., Williams, A.R., *et al.* (2023). Prevalence and characteristics of Autism Spectrum Disorder among children aged 8 years—Autism and Developmental Disabilities Monitoring Network." MMWR. *Surveillance Summaries*, 72(2), 1–14. www.cdc.gov/mmwr/volumes/72/ss/ss7202a1.htm.

7 Chasnoff, I. J., Wells, A. M., & King, L. (2015). Misdiagnosis and missed diagnoses in foster and adopted children with prenatal alcohol exposure. *Pediatrics*, 135(2), 264–270. https://doi.org/10.1542/peds.2014-2171.

8 Dias, B. G. & Ressler, K. J. (2014). Parental olfactory experience influences behavior and neural structure in subsequent generations. *Nature Neuroscience*, 17(1), 89–96.

Chapter 4

1 Wozniak, J. R., Muetzel, R. L., Mueller, B. A., McGee, C. L., *et al.* (2009). Microstructural corpus callosum anomalies in children with prenatal alcohol exposure: An extension of previous diffusion tensor imaging findings. *Alcoholism: Clinical and Experimental Research*, 33(10), 1825–1835. https://doi.org/10.1111/j.1530-0277.2009.01021.x.

2 Ghazi Sherbaf, F., Aarabi, M. H., Hosein Yazdi, M., & Haghshomar, M. (2019). White matter microstructure in fetal alcohol spectrum disorders: A systematic review of diffusion tensor imaging studies. *Human Brain Mapping*, 40(3), 1017–1036. https://doi.org/10.1002/hbm.24409.

3 How Difficult Can This Be—The F.A.T. City Workshop on Youtube. https://youtu.be/Q3UNdbxk3xs?si=_poTL9Cgadh5UJFw.

Chapter 5

1 Forbes, H. T. & Post, B. (2009). *Beyond Consequences, Logic, and Control : A Love-Based Approach to Helping Attachment-Challenged Children with Severe Behaviors*. Beyond Consequences Institute.

2 Bruce Perry's Neurosequential Model: www.neurosequential.com.

3 Trust-Based Relational Intervention (TBRI). https://child.tcu.edu/about-us/tbri/#sthash.dXSfcp3q.dpbs.

4 Delahooke, M. (2019). *Beyond Behaviors: Using Brain Science and Compassion to Understand and Solve Children's Behavioral Challenges*. Pesi Publishers.

5 Delahooke, M. (2022). *Brain–Body Parenting: How to Stop Managing Behavior and Start Raising Joyful, Resilient Kids*. HarperCollins.

6 Cuartas, J., Weissman, D. G., Sheridan, M. A., Lengua, L., & McLaughlin, K. A. (2021). Corporal punishment and elevated neural response to threat in children. *Child Development*, 92, 821–832. https://doi.org/10.1111/cdev.13565.

Chapter 6

1 Diane Malbin, FASCETS Neurobehavioral Model. https://fascets.org.

Acknowledgments

For two decades, people have told me to write a book, and I always laughed it off. Writing has never been my passion—my strength lies in speaking and training. When Stephen Jones, my editor at Jessica Kingsley Publishers, reached out about writing this book, I delayed him for as long as I could. His patience and support throughout this process have been unwavering, even when, a month before the deadline, he kindly asked if I needed more time (to which I emphatically responded NO, knowing my tendency to procrastinate). Stephen, I truly appreciate your encouragement and understanding.

To my husband, Michael, thank you for your patience—especially during those last two months when I pulled at least seven all-nighters to finish writing. I'm sure I snapped at you more than I should have, but you never wavered. You even put up with my slightly embarrassing habit of watching Hallmark movies while I wrote. I need background noise, but music distracts me, and if I put on a show I love, I'll get sucked in. Hallmark movies, though, are predictable—I can tune in and out without getting distracted. So, thank you for enduring that too.

My children have been incredibly supportive of this project, especially Akila, the focus of this book. Thank you, Akila—you are amazing. To Imani, Hezekiah, and Zeke, you inspire me every day. I acknowledge the challenges you faced growing up and how Dad and

I didn't always get it right. Your patience and love mean everything. And to Mowgli, you are forever part of our family—I love you, son.

To my Florida bestie, Wendy Ackerman: you spent countless hours listening to my webinars and transcribing them so I could adapt the material for this book. I hope your hands survived the marathon typing sessions! You are the definition of a great friend.

To Toni Chelikowsky, your offer to edit this book was a lifesaver. Your attention to detail and ability to catch my quirky writing habits made this process so much easier. I am forever grateful for your generosity and expertise.

To Christine Beaufencamp and Laurie Anderson, my fellow FASD coaches, thank you for your invaluable insights and feedback. And to Rebecca Tillou, an adult with FASD, thank you for sharing your perspective over the past year—I have learned so much from you.

To Julie Martindale, our late-night nachos and diet soda sessions are some of my favorite memories and were a lifeline during some of the most stressful seasons. Thank you for always being there.

To Katherin Hui Gregorovic, thank you for the amazing graphic showing the difference between fair and equal. Your art–and your humor–inspire me all the time.

To the incredible staff at Akila's group home, especially Abol Barnaba, I am deeply grateful for your care and dedication. And to Akila's legal guardian, Lori Wirtzfeld, thank you for being someone I can trust wholeheartedly with my daughter's well-being. Finding professionals who genuinely care and whom you can rely on is rare and priceless—so please Abol and Lori, don't think about retiring anytime soon (just kidding...mostly).

There are a few others who paved the way for me and deserve my deepest gratitude. Kari Fletcher, the first FASD trainer I ever heard, had a profound impact on me. Besides Akila and the youth I've worked with, Kari has taught me more than anyone else in this world. Her expertise in connected relational parenting continues to inspire me, and I am forever grateful for her guidance.

Jodee and Liz Kulp have also been incredible teachers through their books and other projects. Liz's passing last year was a tremendous loss to our FASD community, but her spirit and lessons live on. She was a beautiful soul, and her mother, Jodee, is continuing her legacy in remarkable ways.